W0017893

For Rick & Salomea
with Blessings,
Dale

Practical Yoga Sūtras

Practical Yoga Sūtras

by

Dale M. Buegel, M.D. E-RYT 500

Published by

Vitality Matters, LLC

ISBN: 978-1-63192-421-7

Vitality Matters, LLC
1600 W. Green Tree Road, #312
Glendale, WI, 53209
U.S.A.

I dedicate this book to my teacher, who consciously left his body in November, 1996. He was known in the West as Swami Rama of the Himalayas. In India he was known by various names, Bhole Baba, Bhole Prabu, Dandi Swami Sadashiva Bharati, to name a few. Some claim that in older times he was known as Swami Rama Tirtha and in more ancient times by a Biblical name.

I asked Swami Rama to be taught in silence. I wanted to actually experience what is written about in ancient texts like the Yoga Sūtras. I did not wish to simply read the texts or hear lectures about them. Swami Rama was very generous in facilitating my growth on the path of yoga, and for that I am grateful.

"You are the architect of your life and you decide your destiny."

Swami Rama

Contents

Samādhi Pāda

Sādhanā Pāda

Vibhūti Pāda

Kaivalya Pāda

Glossary of Sanskrit Terms

Practices Contained in the Text

Samādhi Pada

I.	Feeling the dance between the "ha" and the "tha" between the air flows of the nostrils
II.	Challenging the mind to maintain continuous focus
III.	Exploring the tastes of foods
IV.	Changing one's identity
V.	Watching the mind modify its content
X.	Studying the space between thoughts
XII.	Handling mistakes in life
XIII.	Diaphragmatic breathing with "soham"
XV.	Fulfilling one's desires on the path of yoga
XXIII.	Doing your meditation in the presence of the Divine
XXVII.	Chanting "AUM"
XXVIII.	Practice of "soham" where the streams of coolness join
XXXVIII.	Yoga nidrā
XLI.	Pretending to be the Divine

Sādhanā Pāda

III.	Contemplating the experience after death
XXI.	Contemplating experience as a divine gift
XXII.	Practices of love
XXXII.	Dealing with grief and shame
	Dealing with fears
	Contemplation on presence of the Divine
XXXIII.	Contemplating opposites
XLVI.	Finding barriers of restriction in āsana practice
XLVII.	Practicing steadiness in standing pose
XLIX.	Nādī ṣodhana
	Focusing on prāṇa flows between the nostrils
	Focusing on nostril dominance in āsanas
L.	Preparation for breath retention
LIV.	AUM kriya

Vibhūti Pāda

II.	Meditation on “soham” at anāhata cakra
X.	Letting the mind dwell in the silence
XXVI.	Building tactile sensitivity and feeling the cakras
XXXII.	Locating kūrma nādī

Preface

Within each of us lies the capacity to know all things. But, how do we gather the experiences that teach us? That is the question. Humanity has well demonstrated its thirst to explore the physical world, traveling across oceans past many fears in rickety crafts, facing dangers of the wild to discover new territory, pushing out into space to look for new worlds and races of beings, and diving deep into the oceans, wondering what lies hidden there.

There is one frontier that has mystified us since the beginning of time. Who are we? From where do we arise? Why are we here? How can we know who or what gave origin to us? We search in books, ask questions of those we consider wiser than ourselves, observe our lives, and still puzzle over these questions.

Religions and philosophies of the world tell us that the Divine is everywhere, including the permeation of each and every part of each and every one of us. How do we know this? How do we touch the Divine with our awareness and experience this? How do we experience this Divine as truth?

Within the heart of each human being lies not only the ache to know the answers to these questions, but also the means to find these answers. Throughout history sages in all the religious and philosophical traditions have taught methods of contemplation, prayer, and meditation to help us explore the limitless inner frontier of awareness.

While exploring the sacred space within ourselves, some interesting side effects occur. Health benefits, joy, harmony and well-being can all unfold. Other side effects include challenges to our cherished habits of thinking and being in the world. Just as we had to give up preconceived notions of the world being flat, we must give up preconceived notions about our true nature and travel beyond the ocean of ignorance that lies within us.

In this book we will explore concepts of who we are and what practical things we can do to discover the truths of our inner frontier. Some of the concepts and methods may be familiar, and some might seem odd. Please assimilate and accept that which makes sense and can be verified by experience, and let go for now of that which the heart and mind cannot both agree to practice or receive.

One ancient text that addresses the questions of humanity and the process through which answers to the questions of our being can be obtained is the Yoga Sūtras. It is a text summarizing a path in life that can lead to the goal of knowledge of all things. The Yoga Sūtras, descriptive threads (sūtras), were likely passed from teacher to student orally long before they were written. As with many of the texts of old, the Yoga Sūtras were written for those already familiar with yoga practices and not for the uninitiated.

The format of the Yoga Sūtras is four sections called pādas consisting of concise verses summarizing the path and goal of yoga. "Pāda'' is translated as "foot", the four pādas or feet being the support for the body of knowledge called "yoga". The pādas are not written like cookbooks with precise instructions that any beginner could follow in order to produce a cake or a batch of cookies. While many commentaries have been written on the Yoga Sūtras, the goal of this particular commentary is to attempt to make the concepts presented in the original sūtras more accessible to yoga practitioners in this day and age. The practices and suggestions for contemplation added to this commentary on the Yoga Sūtras are those that have been helpful to me in understanding and verifying what is presented by the ancient authors. I am not a Sanskrit scholar. I am a yoga practitioner. The commentary and suggestions in this book are presented from the viewpoint of a practitioner. For those unfamiliar with some of the Sanskrit terms, there is a glossary of terms following the text of the Kaivalya Pada at the end of this book.

Dale M. Buegel, May 4th, 2014

Acknowledgements

I give thanks to my teacher, Swami Rama, who always said I should write more.

I also give thanks to Swami Veda Bharati who introduced me to the teachings of yoga and also introduced me to Swami Rama some four decades ago. Swami Veda also provided me with a framework from which to study the Yoga Sūtras as outlined in the table of contents of this book. I also thank Pandit Rajmani Tigunait who, in addition to Swami Veda, helped with the teaching of some specific practices over the years of my training. I also thank the unmanifest guides that open the gateways of knowledge when the time is correct to do so.

In addition I thank my students for continually challenging me to find ways to present the subject of yoga in a practical format. I specifically thank Jamie Lynn Tatera for suggestions regarding the format of this book and for copy editing. I also thank Michaela Feriancikova for allowing me to use photographs of her to illustrate some specific practices.

I thank my wife, Ragani, for encouraging me (for years) to finally write this book.

Samādhi Pāda

I. Now begins the exposition of yoga.

Preceding the "Now", it is assumed that the reader has done a considerable amount of yoga practice in order to be able to understand what follows in this text of the Yoga Sūtras. The "exposition" of yoga is actually to be done by the student through the results of their own yoga practice. While one can read the words of the sūtras, understanding will only come through practice and the grace of insight that dawns when the student is fully prepared to experience those states of consciousness spoken about in the Yoga Sūtras.

The meaning of the word "yoga" can be translated as union, or of binding together. Some think of yoga as the binding of body, mind, and spirit with the Divine. This is similar in meaning to the root word of "religion", namely the Latin word *religio*, which also means to bind together.

Practices:

From the standpoint of yoga practices, the term "yoga" has several practical meanings of union, or binding together. My teacher helped me experience two of those meanings. The term "hatha yoga" means the union or binding together of the "ha" and the "tha", the solar and lunar energies, the right and the left energy channels of piṅgalā and iḍā. The right and left energies dance with each other side to side continuously in ordinary states of consciousness. Initially I was taught to experience this energetic dance in the quiet space between the air flows of each nostril. If one attends to the coolness in each nostril during inhalation and the warmth in each nostril during exhalation, one can define two separate air flows, one in each nostril. Looking between those two air flows one can find a space where there is no airflow. In that space between the flows can be felt the energetic dance between the left and the right. The dance was first described to me as the eddy of water behind the tail of a large fish as it slowly swims through the water.

Once I could feel the dance in that quiet space, I was then taught to feel the side to side energetic dance moving through the bony part of the nose bridge. Additionally I was instructed to feel the dance between the orbits of the eye sockets which are connected to the energetic petals of ājñā cakra. I was also taught to feel the dance between piṅgalā and iḍā at the indentation above the upper lip, which rests between the right and left prominences of the upper lip. This energetic dance can be felt at any level in the system of cakras, but for many, is more easily felt at ājñā cakra. When the dance comes to stillness, one is able to open a central channel of energy, suṣumnā, which allows one to experience expanded states of awareness. The practices of hatha yoga, prāṇayāma and āsana in particular, are designed to produce a union, a silence of the dance between the "ha" and the "tha".

Another practical meaning of union or binding together concerns the energetic flows of prāṇa and apāṇa, the upward flow and the downward flow of energy that follows the rhythm of the breath. My teacher said the first thing that students in the caves are taught is how to die. I did not understand that statement until I was allowed to experience the union of prāṇa and apāṇa in the presence of my teacher. Binding these two energy flows together to produce stillness can result in a state called kevala kumbhaka, a mystical state similar to a near-death experience where the need to breathe can be suspended for an indefinite period of time. Unlike a near-death experience, however, medical risk is not required.

Something to consider:

One can read the words about the practices above and contemplate their meaning. Alternatively, one can choose to do the practices and observe the results. One must consider whether now is the time in life to begin such practices? When students would ask my teacher how many lifetimes of yoga practice it would take them in order to experience the state of samādhi, he would say "Why not now, in this lifetime?" Are you ready to experience the Divine in this lifetime, or are you content to wait until death and beyond to potentially have that experience? Do you wish to know your history before you transitioned into this life? Do you wish to understand that creative force which gave rise to you? Before you die do you wish to know where your consciousness will go after death?

II. Yoga is inhibition or restraint of the modifications of the mind.

The sages of many mystical traditions tell us that it is worthwhile to bring our minds to silence. To understand the importance of that silent state of mind, it is helpful to examine the origin and the makeup of the mind. Below is a diagram drawn by my teacher in many of his lectures depicting connections between the soul, mind, kuṇḍalinī, prāṇa, and the body and senses.

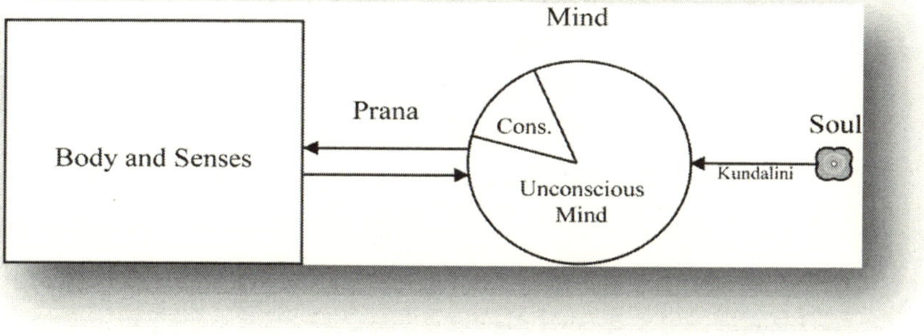

During one of his lectures my teacher was asked to define the soul. He explained that if you take a spark of divine potential and wrap it in layers upon layers of ignorance, you will have a human soul. Those layers of ignorance include the results of one's previous actions, the fruits of one's karma. If you then apply the force of kuṇḍalinī (first prāṇa, Śakti, Divine Mother, Holy Spirit, silver cord) through the layers of ignorance (influenced by past karmas), the mind is created. One's birth circumstance and the obstacles and opportunities that may present themselves in life are, in part, determined by the layers of ignorance that are part of the soul. The energies of prāṇa then further act as an interface between the mind and the body and senses.

One aspect of our minds is citta-vṛitti. This is considered a storehouse of the vibrations of the universe. The physicists of the world will tell us that this book you are currently reading as a printed page or are viewing on a computer screen is merely a collection of molecules. These molecules are made up of atoms. The atoms are made up of particles of atoms. The particles, upon closer examination, are nothing but organizations of energy and vibration of different wavelengths. Depending upon how the energetic vibrations are organized within a particular space, that space can be perceived by our senses in different ways, such as solids, liquids, gases, a printed page, or as virtually anything.

The mystics of different traditions tell us that all phenomena, all events, all objects in the universe have a vibratory nature and that each vibration radiates everywhere in the universe. Every phenomena, event, word uttered, or thought, is projected throughout the entire universe and registered in the mind as a conscious or unconscious experience. If a tree falls in the forest and we are in our homes, the tree falling registers as a subtle vibration in our unconscious. If we are next to the tree when it falls, however, the event of the tree falling can register as a conscious experience and also persist in our memory banks on an unconscious level.

What defines us as individual human beings is the placement of the boundaries between the conscious and unconscious mind. While we may share similar conscious vibrations with another individual, having shared the same experience of being next to the tree when it fell, for example, there are differences in what registers on a conscious level for each human being. The totality of the conscious and unconscious mind, the totality of the circle of the mind in my teacher's diagram, is exactly the same for each and every one of us. It is only the boundaries between conscious and unconscious mind that differ from individual to individual. We are indeed all created equal in that the totality of our mind is the same for each and every one of us. It is our awareness of the boundaries between conscious and unconscious mind that contributes to our perception of ourselves as individuals. That perception of our self as an individual is called ego or ahaṃkāra, our sense of I-am-ness.

This sūtra indicates that one of the paths to achieving yoga, or union with our essential nature as a spark of the Divine, involves quieting the modifications of our mind, leading the mind to silence.

Practices:

To understand something of the nature of the modifications of the mind, do the following practice. Create a sound mentally in the mind that is of a continuous nature. The sound might be that of a vowel or a consonant. For example, "aaaaaaaaaa…", "eeeeeeeeeeeeeeeeee…", "oooooooooooooooooooooo…", "mmmmmmmmmm…" See how long the mind can maintain awareness on the continuous sound before a thought or memory interrupts the focus. Pay attention to which sound the mind is most comfortable maintaining. Different sounds have different vibratory characteristics which may appeal to the mind's focus or might actually be uncomfortable for the mind to maintain over time. One of the principles of mantra meditation is to use the vibratory nature of sound created in the mind to groove the focus of the mind.

Try to maintain silence in the mind for more than a few seconds. See how long your mind is content to remain silent.

Listen to some music and observe how long it takes your mind to wander. Does the quality or genre of music make a difference in the ability of the music to influence the focus of your mind?

Something to consider:

How much control of your mind do you consciously have? How much control of your conscious mind do you wish to have?

III. Then the seer is established in his own essential and fundamental nature.

As the following sūtras will describe, there are different ways of knowing. Once the modifications of the mind are restrained, a different way of understanding becomes possible.

If we wish to build a house, we will perhaps sketch out a design that appeals to us with the number, shape, and size of rooms, etc. We might engage an architect to translate our dream house into a workable diagram. We will get an idea of how many bricks, boards, nails, etc. are needed to actually build the house. We will investigate financing, possible locations, and make decisions along the way about how best to proceed. In the process we would gain a deeper understanding of the meaning of the word "house."

While this kind of a deductive process is very useful for building a house, it is less useful when trying to understand our essential nature and the divine spark from which we arise. The sages recognize there are different ways to know things. One way is to personally experience that which one is trying to understand. One can gather 1000 descriptions from 1000 people about what it was like to taste sugar. One might also simply make the sugar part of oneself by tasting and taking the sugar into oneself, thereby gathering the experiential knowledge of how sugar tastes.

One of the goals of yoga practice is to attain the ability to gain intuitive knowledge without the intermediary steps of data gathering and deductive reasoning. The quieting of the mind with its modifications allows one the opportunity to merge awareness with that which one is trying to understand and experience the object of study as that object of study experiences itself. In order to successfully accomplish a state of consciousness which allows such merging, one must be able to surrender the sense of I-am-ness. The mind also needs to be without any activity or waves in order for the mind to become one with its object of study. The absence of prior impressions allows the mind to be in an unbiased, fresh state before merging with an object of study. Rather than depend upon the thousands of descriptions offered in the literature of the world about the characteristics of the Divine, the yogis choose to quiet the modifications of the mind and experience the Divine directly by becoming consciously merged with the Divine.

Practice:

Choose a food that you have not yet tasted in life. This may take some research. Gather some descriptions of the nature of that food, where it or its ingredients come from, descriptions of its taste, its potential medicinal effects, etc. Once the research has been done, contemplate in the mind what that food might actually taste like. Create the actual taste in your mind if you can. Then find or prepare the food and actually taste it. Compare the image in the mind from the research done to the actual taste experienced once the food is consumed.

A simpler, less time-consuming practice is to choose food whose taste is already known to you. Chew that food carefully a full thirty times and experience the changes in flavor that might occur.

Something to consider:

Consider that the knowledge obtained through analysis of gathered data is different than the knowledge gained through actual experience. Are you content to read descriptions of that aspect of the Divine within you, or do you wish to merge your awareness with the Divine to fully experience that aspect of yourself? Are you content with the knowledge that you have already gathered in life, or do you wish to know more?

IV. In other states (non-yoga states) there is assimilation of the seer with the modifications of the mind.

One can identify oneself with the image of oneself, such as looking in the mirror and saying "That's me." One can see oneself as black or white, tall or short, as parent or child, as husband or wife, or define oneself with many concepts, labels, or images.

Practice:

If you have pets, engage the pet as the pet would attempt to engage you. Mirror the pet's mannerisms, sounds, and behaviors. When my horse was eating a flake of hay in the arena, I would paw the ground as if I were looking for food. The horse would separate a portion of the hay with her hoof and nuzzle it in my direction so that I might also have food.

Another practice is to take on a different identity for a period of time. Exchange roles with a member of your household for a few hours or for a day. Share the experience with your household member of what that change in role was like for you.

Something to consider:

Contemplate what part of yourself remained relatively constant during the role changes of the above practices. Consider that there is an aspect of yourself that is not limited by a defined role or by limitations of conscious knowledge.

V. Five-fold modifications of the mind, painful and not painful.

The vṛittis, modifications of the mind, are defined in the following sūtras to be of five types. This sūtra states that various modifications of the mind in response to incoming data can be painful or not painful. Not painful would be neutral or pleasurable. The following are some examples. If one is in traffic most vehicles pass by unnoticed. The perception of these vehicles does not register with enough energy or affect (emotional feeling) to have much of an impact on our minds. Their passage is quickly forgotten and relegated to the unconscious as a neutral modification of the mind. If a vehicle and driver behave in a manner that makes us angry, there may be more affect and energy attached and registered in our mind as an unpleasant experience. Another example is when we might see a vehicle that particularly appeals to us and that we then desire to have. While seeing the object may initially produce a pleasurable impression, the unfulfilled desire might cause us to feel some level of pain.

Practice:

Find an object in your surroundings that you had not previously noticed and take the time to gaze at it for a minute or two. Does the object continue to remain neutral to you? Do feelings arise? Does the mind tire of this concentration and move the focus of attention somewhere else?

Next, remember an experience or person that you have been particularly thankful to have had in your life. After creating that image of remembered well-being in the mind, bring your focus to the area of your body where the lower ribs join the breastbone near the heart while letting your breath become slow and smooth (The practice of this diaphragmatic breath is found in the commentary on sūtra XIII.) Does the energy the mind associates with the image change when you bring the focus near the heart center? Do the feelings strengthen or change?

Something to consider:

Can attending to a content of mind with interest alter the neutrality of that particular content of mind? Can engaging the energy of a particular energy center (cakra) also change the energy and affect associated with a particular content of mind?

VI. The five-fold modifications are: right knowledge, wrong knowledge, fancy, sleep, and memory.

These classes of modifications of the mind will be explained in the following sūtras.

VII. Right knowledge is based on direct cognition, inference, and tested and attested facts.

Some knowledge is deductive in nature. We analyze a set of data and draw conclusions. We consider those conclusions to then be true. Court cases are full of exhibits and facts that are attested to by both sides. Because the facts are generally attested to they are considered to be true. Research is full of hypotheses that are tested. If the hypothesis is supported by the research, there develops a faith that the hypothesis is true.

Scriptures that contain knowledge that is widely accepted by a particular group may also be considered attested facts, that group having faith in a particular scripture. Where there is faith, however, without direct experience of what is presented in the scripture, there may still be some lingering doubt as to whether everything in the scripture is considered right knowledge. Direct experience leading to belief can be considered right knowledge by a practitioner because it results from direct cognition.

Some knowledge is based on inference. If we hear the sound of a bird singing outside our window, we assume that the bird is there. This may be because of our past experience of having seen a bird singing that same song outside our window.

Something to consider:

At one time in human history the world was considered to be flat. People walked the earth and it seemed flat to them. Not realizing their experience of the world was quite limited, people assumed the entire world to be flat. As more data was collected through experience, the attested fact of the world being flat changed to the attested fact that the world is a sphere. Perhaps there is much more to be learned about the true nature of the world as more direct experience is yet to be gathered.

VIII. Wrong knowledge is a lack of correspondence between perception and fact.

One might see a mirage of a mountain range or a city while traveling across the desert that appears to be a short distance ahead. If no such city or mountain range exists, this would be considered wrong knowledge as the perception of the city or mountain range does not correlate with fact. Also, there may be such a city or mountain range whose image has been bent to appear in the mirage at a much closer distance than where that city or mountain range actually is located. Both perceptions are examples of wrong knowledge.

IX. Fancy-imagination.

One might conjure up an image in the mind when hearing a story told. A friend might want to introduce you to someone they have described, and an image appears in the mind of what that person might look like. One might hear a description of the Divine and develop an image of how the Divine might appear when perceived with the senses. All are examples of imagination producing an image in our mind.

Something to consider:

Can a mind with limited experience of the Divine conjure up an accurate image of the Divine? Can the Divine be accurately described and portrayed to others?

X. Nidrā: no content of mind.

While nidrā is generally translated as sleep and the content of mind considered to be absent from consciousness, the yogis explore a state called yoga nidrā where the content of the mind that would ordinarily remain unconscious during the state of sleep is brought into consciousness. Nidrā in the context of this sūtra, however, means nothing is occupying the focus of the mind. Such a state may be momentary, such as the space between thoughts, or extended, as in some meditative states.

Practice:

Recline or lie quietly and attempt to study the mind's transitions. How does the mind move from one thought, sense perception, or feeling to the next? Is there any perceivable space between contents of the mind that is without thought, sensory perception, or feeling? Can that space between contents of the mind be extended through will?

Something to consider:

Voluntary control of the mind through the application of our will can be difficult. Sometimes the simplest of practices can be the most difficult practices in yoga for us master.

XI. Memory: not allowing an object which has been experienced to escape.

Memory has five components. For any event in the universe there is the knowledge of what happened that registers on either a conscious or an unconscious level. If a tree that falls over in the forest is observed to fall, the event registers on a conscious level and will still be present in one's unconscious memory bank even after the original event is forgotten.

There may be a behavior associated with the event. For example one may have had to jump out of the way of the falling tree. This behavioral component also registers initially on a conscious and later on an unconscious level. If one experienced fear that the tree falling might cause harm, then that feeling or affect will also register on a conscious and unconscious level. A tightening or grabbing sensation in the gut might accompany the fear. In addition to a visceral response to emotion, if one was actually hit by the tree there may be pain also associated with the experience as a bodily sensation.

Each event in the universe also has a prāṇic or vibratory component associated with it. The level of focus at the time of an event contributes to the amplitude of that vibratory, energetic component. In the above example, fear may have intensified one's concentration on the event of the tree falling.

An acronym, BAKES, for the components of memory is as follows:

B-behavior associated with the event.

A-affect associated with the event.

K-knowledge of what happened.

E-energetic component associated with the event.

S-bodily sensations associated with the event.

It is primarily the affect and energetic components associated with a memory that determines whether that event will continue to push forward in the mind and influence such states of the mind as a dream, conscious thinking, or one's meditation.

Something to consider:

What role do memories play in determining what emerges into the mind's conscious awareness when the practitioner attempts to quiet the mind?

XII. Cessation of the waves of the mind is brought about by persistent practice and nonattachment to the waves of the mind and its modifications.

Decreasing the amount of energy and affect associated with a particular event in the mind is an aspect of nonattachment. This can be helpful in reducing the pressure of that particular event to be a continuing influence on a conscious and unconscious level.

Practice:

If one feels one has made a mistake in life that one continues to grieve over or have continuing and recurrent feelings of regret, it is necessary to reduce the attachment to that event in order to resolve its continuing influence on the mind. One strategy to handle mistakes suggested in one of my teacher's lectures is to contemplate what one needed to learn from that mistake. Once the lesson is learned, one can make restitution for that mistake if that seems in order, and then let go of the attached feelings and energy associated with grief and regret. Remaining feelings regarding the incident were to be offered into the light and fire of the Divine. My teacher also noted there are no coincidences or accidents in life. The guiding force of this universe observes every mistake we make and continues to lovingly offer us opportunities in life to learn. If the Divine can forgive us for our mistakes, then we must also learn to forgive ourselves for our mistakes if we ever hope to merge our awareness with the Divine.

Something to consider:

Do people who make no mistakes in life really need to be born? Is there anything here in life for them to learn?

XIII. Abhyāsa: the effort to become firmly established in citta-vṛitti-nirodha, silence of the fluctuations of the mind.

This verse of the sūtras states that one must make effort in one's practice to succeed in establishing and maintaining the state of citta-vṛitti-nirodha.

Practice:

One of the simpler yoga practices to train the mind to achieve steady focus without fluctuation is diaphragmatic breathing. This practice has several key components:

1. Relax the secondary muscles of breathing, those muscles located between the ribs as well as the muscles located in the neck.

2. As you inhale, the diaphragm (the large muscle that separates the abdominal cavity from the lung cavity) contracts. As it contracts the muscle thickens and flattens, expanding the lung cavity to take in air and exerting pressure against the abdominal contents. The abdominal muscles are relaxed to allow full expansion of the belly.

3. As you exhale, the navel is drawn posteriorly toward the spine. Even when you are lying on your back, use

conscious effort to draw the navel toward the spine in a smooth, controlled fashion.

4. Always keep the mind on the breath. As soon as the breath fluctuates or pauses, the mind also has the opportunity to fluctuate and change the content of the mind. Making the breath smooth and continuous is a way to train the mind to maintain its focus on a single content of mind without fluctuation.

5. Slow the pace of the breath to help it become smooth and even. Do not slow the breath to such an extent that you feel like you need more air.

6. Eliminating the pauses between the breaths is difficult in the beginning. The following are two strategies for mastering the pauses between inhalation and exhalation and between exhalation and inhalation.

   a. To master the pause between inhalation and exhalation, get some experience feeling the full contraction of the diaphragm. When you feel the diaphragm has contracted fully, inhale more. Do this one or two more times until you experience the ability of the diaphragm muscle to fully contract. The belly should become as big as it can become. Be aware that if you fully contract a muscle to the end of its range, that muscle can become slightly tremulous. The diaphragm muscle is no different than other muscles in this regard. You might feel a sensation of tremulousness in the area of the lower rib cage. Another tendency that restricts full diaphragmatic inhalation is the tendency to hold tension in the lower ribs, not allowing the lower rib cage to widen enough to allow full expansion of the belly. Be aware that anatomically there is a portion of the diaphragm that will actually flare out the lower ribs when the diaphragm is fully contracted. With full diaphragmatic contraction, the breath becomes extremely fine in nature and the transition between inhalation and exhalation can be made without the slightest pause.

b. Mastering the pause between exhalation and inhalation requires more subtle perception. It is almost as if the contraction of the diaphragm initiates inhalation before exhalation ends. A subtle energetic wave signals the transition between exhalation and inhalation. This energetic wave can be felt in the lower belly between the level of the navel and the pelvic floor. It is the transition between the descending energy of apāṇa and the ascending energy of prāṇa in that region. The sensation somewhat resembles the activity of an ocean wave gently approaching a beach. The edge of the wave makes its way up the beach, but if you have your leg in the water, you can feel the movement of water underneath the surface already flowing outward towards the open sea.

7. If the mind tends to wander during the practice, you can have the mind create a sound or mantra upon which to focus. The mantra that many of the yoga traditions use for this purpose is "soham (pronounce so-hum)." The sound "sooo...." is created in the mind on the inhale, and the sound "haaaam…." or "hammmm…." on the exhale. If you wish to deepen the practice with this mantra, learn to make the transitions between each consonant and vowel in the mantra smooth, including the transition between the "o" and the "h" as well as between the "m" and the "s".

As we will see later in this text, the practice of attending to transitions will be helpful in learning to establish the states of awareness called samādhi. My teacher used to say that if one could perfectly master the practice of diaphragmatic breathing, one could establish any state of awareness that one chose.

XIV. Abhyāsa (practice) becomes firmly established after being continued for a long time without interruption and when performed with earnestness.

One cannot expect to attain the goal of yoga if one's practice of yoga is intermittent and haphazard.

XV. Vairāgya is the second means to bring about citta-vṛitti-nirodha.

Vairāgya refers to cessation of desire on both a conscious as well as an unconscious level. There are only two ways by which a desire can be resolved. One either has to fulfill the desire or the energy and affect associated with the desire in the mind has to diminish to the point where the desire is no longer present. Fulfilling the desire has the risk of increasing the energy attached to that desire. Not fulfilling the desire also has that same potential risk.

Practices:

Cravings can be strong, such as the desire for sweets, wealth, alcohol, sex, etc. Denying that which is desired can take just as much energy if not more energy than actually fulfilling the desire. If one is still thinking about that which is craved while denying fulfillment of the desire, citta-vṛitti-nirodha has still not been achieved. The energy and feelings associated with the desire are still strong and still create fluctuations in the mind preventing the goal of yoga from being reached.

The solution recommended by some sages is to fulfill one's desires in ways that actually serve others. For example, if one desires wealth, use some of that wealth in the service of others. In the process of gathering that wealth, consider engaging in win-win scenarios where both parties engaged in a business transaction benefit rather than engaging in business in a predatory manner.

My teacher had the capacity to be at peace in any manner of dwelling in which he was situated. He was able to continue to do his work in the service of others regardless of circumstance. Be it while living in a cave in the mountains, a humble apartment dwelling, or surroundings with the trappings of wealth, he was equally at home. If someone admired the shawl he was wearing, he would offer it to them. If someone gave him a house, he would pass it on when it was time for him to work elsewhere.

Another means to master vairāgya is to allow the bliss that occurs when one approaches the light of the Divine to make the energy of attraction dissipate for all else. Even a small glimpse of that bliss in meditation is enough to modify the energy of attachment to one's desires.

Something to consider:

How do your desires serve you in life?

XVI. When there is cessation of the least desire for the guṇas (tendencies that are part of the process of creation), no longer a desire to be separate from the Divine, all desires cease.

When this level of vairāgya is achieved, there is no longer a desire to be born. Still one might choose to be born to do so in the service of others.

When my teacher was younger he went into a cave to meditate for a year. He could not even stand up in the cave. There was an opening through which food could be passed in and waste passed out. There was a small hole to allow light to enter the cave. After a year had passed, he felt he had learned much. He was in a serene state of mind after he exited the cave and approached his master. His master put a foot on my teacher's chest and kicked my teacher down the hill. My teacher was angry and asked his master why he had been kicked down the hill. His master pointed out how angry my teacher had become at such little provocation and asked my teacher what had really been learned during the time spent in the cave.

Something to consider:

My teacher would say that the real mastery of yoga occurs when one is able to keep one's awareness in that bliss of the Divine yet still be functional and able to do one's work in the world.

XVII. Saṃprajñāta samādhi is that form of samādhi that is accompanied by reasoning, reflection, bliss and a sense of pure being or I-am-ness.

In this form of samādhi an object of attraction for the mind is still present. As one's consciousness proceeds toward the expanded state of consciousness called samādhi, the focus of the mind goes through various stages:

1. In the vitarka stage the mind might focus on a gross or concrete object perceivable with the senses. An example would be focusing on an image such as a maṇḍala or a diagram of a cakra. In the state of samādhi the object and all the subtleties become the pratyaya ("seed" or content of the mind at a given moment). This stage however, is not

simply seeing the image of the maṇḍala, but involves the expansion of awareness to have complete and comprehensive understanding of the object of focus. One might understand the reasoning behind the creation of a particular maṇḍala or diagram.

2. The vicāra stage is where the mind might focus on a more subtle content of mind, such as the concept of truth, beauty, goodness, redness, or blueness, etc. As in the vitarka stage, the vicāra stage of samādhi allows complete understanding of the object of focus, and not merely cognitive contemplation of that object of focus. In this stage of samādhi the object of focus is abstract, not concrete.

3. Sānanda samādhi involves expanding one's awareness of the bliss itself. There is only the bliss, not reasoning or reflection as in the previous two types of samādhi.

4. Sasmitā samādhi involves expanding one's awareness of one's pure being or I-am-ness. While there are still seeds in the mind with energy capable of pushing those seeds forward, in the state of sasmitā samādhi, one is only focused upon the pure being.

XVIII. Asaṃprajñāta samādhi is the cloudy remnant impression left in the mind on the dropping of the object of focus in the previous practice.

The state of asaṃprajñāta samādhi can be thought of as a transition state between the four stages of samādhi in the previous sūtra. It is also sometimes translated as samādhi without an object of focus.

There is a practical way to classify the states of samādhi. The four different types of samādhi as taught to me by my teacher are as follows:

1. Samādhi can be with ahaṃkāra (I-am-ness or sense of self) or without ahaṃkāra. One's identity can be retained while studying a particular content of the mind. One can also surrender one's sense of identity to allow one's consciousness to merge with a single content of mind in order to gain intuitive understanding of that content of mind. One's own consciousness merges with and becomes that which is studied.

2. The content of mind studied can either be a void (nirbīja samādhi) or the content of mind can be other than a void (the mind contains a bīja, or seed). The former is called nirbīja samādhi (without seed), and the latter is called sabīja samādhi (with seed or content).

Besides presenting the concepts of these four types of samādhi, the lineage of my teacher was also very generous in providing silent examples. I recall walking through the corridor in what was then the therapy wing of the Himalayan Institute in Honesdale, Pennsylvania. As I passed the corner which held the entrance to my teacher's apartment, his voice very clearly came into my mind and asked "Am I your teacher?" Without breaking stride I immediately replied in my mind "yes" and made my way back to my room. I entered my room, closed the door, and lay down on the mat on the floor to do my customary relaxation.

My senses began to withdraw, and the world began to tune out. I had experienced this before and knew that a state of samādhi was imminent. However, on this occasion, there was a knock on the door that interrupted the transition. I answered the door to a person who was eager to tell me that there was a meeting taking place about some controversy about my teacher, and asked me if I wished to attend. I told him "I know who my teacher is.", and then quickly closed the door in order to get back to my relaxation. Within seconds of lying back down, the world tuned out, and the living image of my teacher's teacher appeared in my mind. What I witnessed was a historical figure familiar to the world gazing at me. I was surprised and attempted to mutter some sort of greeting in my mind. Though I had seen faces gazing at me before in my meditation, I did not realize the significance of their silence. I maintained my sense of self in meditation, rather than surrendering it. While the figure directed my gaze downward, allowing me to experience something of the nature of a luminous glowing lingam, I felt I might have learned much more had I not maintained my identity during that experience. While at one time I regretted not surrendering my sense of I-am-ness during this experience, I now understand that my training was to include experiencing the four different forms of samādhi that my teacher had explained earlier in our relationship.

The second experience that involved the appearance of a guide taught me what might be possible if one can manage to surrender one's sense of identity in order to experience what a guide experiences instead of simply observing. When I was young I had seen a movie, the name of which I no longer recall. I do remember the actor, Sal Mineo, playing a Lakota brave who experienced a vision that I recall was termed wakan tanka associated with a vision of a White Buffalo.

I had just come home from the hospital after gallbladder surgery and still had a drain in my abdomen. I was adjusting myself to lie on my back in the bed when my senses began to tune out once again, signaling an experience of samādhi was forthcoming. My wife asked if I was all right, and I gently motioned her to be quiet. As the world tuned out, I became aware of maṇipūra cakra. Booming into my consciousness resonated the intense vibration of a mantra called mahā-mṛtyuṇjaya mantra. After several powerful spontaneous intonations of that mantra, maṇipūra cakra opened to allow a brilliant white light full of energy to be poured into my navel. It was as if someone had poured the energy and light of the sun into my belly. Not long before this experience I had finished the practice of more than 300,000 repetitions of mahā-mṛtyuṇjaya during the course of my meditation practice.

Following the energy being poured into me, a guide appeared in the form of a buffalo. Different cultures might see the guide of maṇipūra cakra in different forms. In India, it might appear in the form of a ram, but for me it appeared in the form of an American bison. Perhaps this was because I had lived in the area of the Lakota people during my youth. The buffalo was charging, which caused me initially to keep backing away very rapidly. Perhaps because of remembering my previous experience of not joining with the guide and giving up my own sense of identity, I chose to be still and allow the buffalo to charge. As soon as the buffalo reached me, my eyes and senses became the buffalo, charging through the channel of nāḍis until I reached the place where everything was in shades of white. Upon later reflection about this experience, it occurred to me that had I followed and not become the buffalo, I might have seen the White Buffalo in that space where all things appeared in shades of white. I would not have had the experience of joining with the consciousness of a guide to experience the perspective of the guide.

These and other experiences taught me the differences in the four types of samādhi that my teacher had described.

Something to consider:

How will I choose to be when a guide appears in my practice?

XIX. Some confusion of interpretation of this sūtra is evident in the writings of different commentators. The Sūtra describes a class of yogis that may have some attainments but have not completed the path of yoga. They are often reborn with psychic abilities that are easily attained but with non-resolution of the seeds in the mind which continue to influence the individual on both a conscious and unconscious level.

XX. Samādhi for others requires effort and practice. Faith, strength, memory, contemplation (meditation), and discernment are part of that effort and practice.

Faith and strength add to the determination required to reach the goal of yoga. The expansion of awareness termed samādhi is necessary for reaching the goal of yoga. Memory is required to engage in many of the practices of yoga. Many of the practices also involve contemplation and meditation.

Discernment refers to buddhi, that part of consciousness which has the ability to distinguish those aspects of ourselves that are continually fluctuating and changing from that aspect of ourselves which has no need to change. Buddhi allows us to discern that Divine potential (non-dynamic aspect of Self) that combines with the force of creation to become our mind, prāṇas, body, and senses (those aspects of ourselves that are continually changing).

XXI. Practice, practice, practice. Earnestness of the aspirant influences progress.

Something to consider:

My teacher never told me that I had to practice anything. He was also quite clear, however, that not doing practice meant there would be no result.

XXII. Practices have different grades of intensity which can determine progress.

What is intense practice for one practitioner may seem to be moderate practice for another. Each individual has their own capacity for practice, and this capacity can influence the rate of progress on the path of yoga. Attending to one's capacity is also part of the discernment process of yoga, as overextending oneself can actually impede progress along the path of yoga.

XXIII. Iśvara-praṇidhānād vā.

Surrender of self to God, or placing oneself in God is another means to samādhi. Surrendering oneself to a guide that appears during meditation when suṣumnā awareness is established is a form of Iśvara-praṇidhāna. To help cultivate an attitude which can facilitate this joining, it is helpful to engage in practices of bhakti yoga, such as the devotional chanting called kirtan. Surrender of oneself in heartfelt prayer is another practice.

Practice:

Sometime when you're in the mood for it, do your practice as if the Divine is seated next to you watching your progress. It can be a practice of āsana, chanting, breathing, meditation, or contemplation. Then imagine that that divine presence is experiencing every thought, word, and action of your practice, literally having the divine observer within you.

Something to consider:

How would you do your practice differently if you truly realized that the Divine was with you every moment? How would you lead your life differently with that realization?

XXIV. Īśvara is that divine consciousness which is untouched by the afflictions of life. Those afflictions are kleśas (causes of misery), karma (actions), vipāka (fruits of one's actions), and seeds of desire, including the desire for unconsciousness (sleep), or the desire for consciousness that is not yet awakened.

XXV. In the Divine is the highest limit of omniscience.

The highest limit of omniscience can also be thought of as the potential for all things known and as yet to be known.

XXVI. The male aspect of the Divine is he who comes before creation and birth of the lineage.

Potential comes before manifestation. That divine source that is the potential for all things is non-dynamic. It embodies the quality of stillness.

The following figure illustrates the layers of ourselves and their relationship to each other. The figure also illustrates the relationship of our more external layers to that potential that is the source of ourselves.

You can look at your reflection in the mirror and recognize and accept it as being a reflection of your body, part of your own identity. You realize that it is full of physiological and biochemical reactions occurring during every moment in time.

You also recognize that the image changes on a daily basis, and certainly changes over the decades of time.

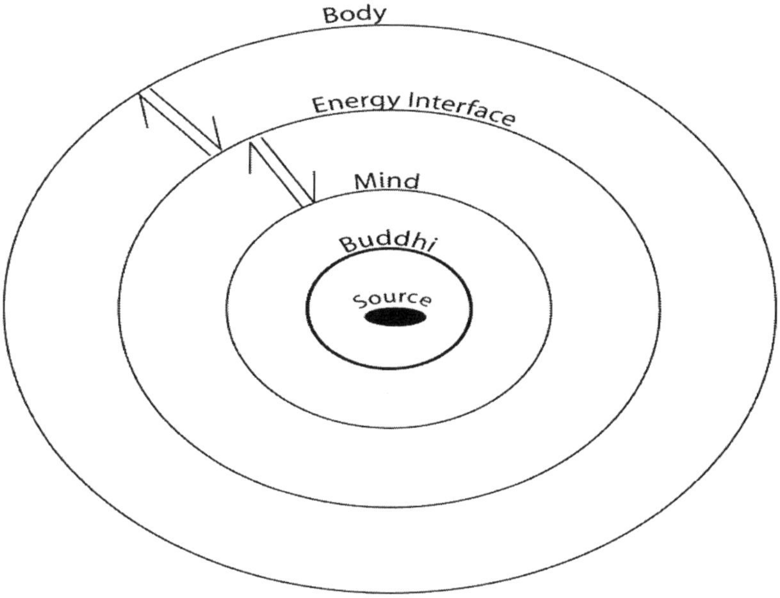

You also accept that your mind has different thoughts and feelings which might change from moment to moment.

Between the mind and body is another aspect of self called prāṇamaya koṣha, the energy interface between mind and body. Medical systems of the world generally accept the existence of this interface and realize that it can be influenced by both mind and body, and can also affect our mind and body. Like the mind and like the body, this interface also fluctuates moment to moment. With a bit of training, you can learn to pick up on this interface with your sense of touch and recognize that this interface has changeable characteristics (practice in Vibhūti Pāda, XXVI).

Giving rise to all of the foregoing aspects of you is the source of yourself, that spark of divine potential with which the force of manifestation unites to create you. The difference between that divine source and the layers of mind, prāṇa, and body is that the divine source is non-dynamic and has no need to change. The more external layers of body, prāṇa, and mind are changing moment to moment. One of the goals of yoga is to develop that aspect of consciousness called buddhi that allows you to discriminate that aspect of yourself that does not change from those aspects of yourself that are constantly changing.

XXVII. God has a designation: vācaka (word expressive) - praṇavaḥ (mystic sound or humming).

Śabdha-Brahman is the primary vibration from which all other vibrations are derived. It is sometimes known as the first prāṇa or kuṇḍalinī, that force that unites with an aspect of divine potential to become a vibration leading to manifestation. The Bible phrases it "In the beginning there was the Word, and the Word was with God, and the Word was God."

In the Vedas, "The name of Brahman is Om, and Om is Brahman himself." Per Swami Satchidananda, the mantra "Om" actually consists of three separate sounds, "A", "U", and "M". The sound "A" is the origination of any sound of any language. It is the sound that is made upon opening the mouth and allowing the first air to pass through the area of the throat where the tongue originates. The sound "U" is a sound that occurs between the origin at the base of the tongue and through the palatal area to the lips. The sound "M" is the vibration that occurs as the lips close. All of the mantras commonly practiced in yoga contain aspects of the mantra "AUM".

Practice:

Establish diaphragmatic breathing and audibly chant the mantra "AUM". Extend each sound of the mantra and lengthen the breath. Pay close attention to the transitions between each sound. Sense where each sound resonates within the body. Change the pitch and see if the locus of resonance changes.

Next chant the mantra silently, still lengthening the breath and attending closely to the transitions between the sounds. The sounds of the mantra need to merge into each other rather than remaining separate. Then extend each sound for more than one breath. Observe the mind's tendency at the end of each inhalation and at the end of each exhalation. Notice whether the locus of the sound's resonance corresponds with any particular area within you.

Something to consider:

Mantras have the capacity to resonate with different aspects of ourselves. The way in which a mantra is practiced affects that resonance.

XXVIII. Japa: having the mind dwell upon its designator reveals that which is designated.

The principle of mantra practice is bhāvanā, dwelling upon in the mind. Sanskrit is a language where the meaning of the word or phrase can be understood by meditating upon the sound and vibration of the word or phrase while expanding one's awareness. The idea is that if one meditates upon the reflection of what one wishes to know and expands one's awareness while maintaining the reflection as the mind's object of focus, one can understand the aspect of reality which produced the reflection. When one practices mantra japa, one continually repeats the sound or vibration of the reflection in the mind to facilitate one-pointed focus upon the reflection.

Mantram is that which keeps the mind steady and produces the proper effect. Each of the five lower cakras from the throat to the root cakra is surrounded by lotus petals. These petals are actually energy centers corresponding to the vibration of each of the Sanskrit vowels and consonants. When one practices mantra japa, one is weaving an energetic pattern to groove the mind. This grooving of the mind facilitates one-pointed focus (an aspect of meditation) that allows one to obtain the higher states of consciousness described by the yogis.

Practice:

Establish diaphragmatic breathing with an erect spine in either a seated or supine (śavāsana) position. Once the smoothness of breath is established, focus on the flow of the breath in the nostrils. Become aware of the coolness in the nostrils during inhalation and the temperature transition to warmth in the nostrils with exhalation. Next focus the awareness of the mind entirely within the right nostril. Find the point in the right nostril that is the absolute coolest during inhalation. Narrow the focal point to the size of a head of a pin. Pay attention to the temperature transitions at that single point in the right nostril. After some time, switch the awareness to the left nostril and find the coolest point in the left nostril. Let the awareness dwell upon the temperature transitions at that point.

After building awareness in each nostril, try to differentiate two streams of coolness with inhalation, one in each nostril. When awareness of the two separate streams of airflow has been established, follow the two streams of coolness to where they join deep in the nasal cavity. Study the temperature transitions at that area of joining, coolness on the inhale transitioning to warmth on the exhale. Try to discover the exact moment of transition between warmth and coolness at the end of each phase of the breath.

Combine the mantra "soham" with the breath, "soooo" on the inhale and "haaammm" on the exhale. Follow the sound in the mind with the breath and make the transitions between each aspect of the sound smooth. Some transitions will be more challenging, such as the transition between “m” and “s”. After focusing in this manner for a time, stop the mental repetition of the mantra and simply listen for the sound of the breath deep in the nasal cavity where the streams of coolness from each nostril join. Gently constrict the vocal cords with each phase of the breath as if you were going to make the sounds of “soooo” and “haaammm” without actually vocalizing the mantra. Listen for the subtle change in the airflow deep in the nasal cavity. It is as if the mantra begins to flow as a whisper with the breath.

XXIX. From the practice (of mantra japa) results the disappearance of the obstacles to perception with unencumbered consciousness or pratyak-cetanā, inward turned consciousness.

What has been described in the previous sūtras is a portion of the path taken to understand and join with the consciousness of the Divine, allowing consciousness to turn inward to that source of ourselves.

XXX. Distractions that prevent the inward turning of the mind include disease, doubt, languor (lack of a definite and dynamic purpose in life), laziness, and desires for worldly things, delusions (false beliefs), failure to progress (non-achievement of a particular stage on the path of yoga), carelessness (including carelessness in one’s practice) , and instability (non-steadiness of mind, emotions, and body).

XXXI. Accompanying these distractions are despair, depression, mental sickness, lack of control over the body, tremulousness, and disturbance of breath.

Something to consider:

My teacher used to say “There is no such thing as failure, only loss of time”. We are created to learn to achieve the goal of yoga. The timing and path chosen vary for each of us.

XXXII. To remove the obstacles, practice one truth or principle.

Some commentators interpret this as adopting one primary practice in yoga and sticking to it no matter what. While it is important to develop the discipline of being able to consistently practice a particular mantra, technique, āsana, or prāṇāyāma, it is also important to note when the result of the practice has been achieved. One can then decide whether to continue that practice or change the routine of one’s yoga practice.

Each student of yoga has different capacities and abilities for practice. These capacities and abilities change over time. As an example, consider the practice of mantra japa. Some mantras may be practiced for a lifetime. However, other mantras are meant to be practiced for a particular period of time and/or for a particular purpose or result. For example one might practice mahāmṛtyuṇjaya mantra to facilitate ease of transitions. These transitions might be as simple as traveling from one place to another, or for easing the travel for a loved one from life into death. One student’s mind may need a longer mantra because of the nature of their mind. A shorter mantra might be more suitable for another student. At some stage on the path of yoga, one may need to change the mantra or add an additional mantra.

Some students do better with a complex practice that can better occupy the mind. The simplest of practices may have more of a tendency to allow distraction of the mind. Focusing on a single continuous sound, such as in some of the practices in the Tantric traditions, can require absolute steadiness of breath and mind to prevent the mind from being its usual rascal, trying to run off in another direction at the first opportunity.

XXXIII. The mind becomes clarified by cultivating attitudes of friendliness toward happiness, compassion toward misery, gladness toward virtue, and indifference toward vice.

The message of this sūtra is about developing clarity of mind in one's attitude towards others. Being indifferent to the qualities of happiness, misery, virtue, and vice allows one to be friendly towards those who are happy, compassionate towards those who are in misery, feel gladness for those who are virtuous, and disregard for those who are wicked. This allows consciousness to keep the mind clear and in control while in contact with the people of the world.

XXXIV. The mind is also clarified by controlled expiration and retention of breath.

Regulation of breath is different than prāṇāyāma as later defined. The yogis recognize a link between breath and mind. Every fluctuation in the breath, every jerk, and every pause provides opportunity for the mind to change focus. Making the breath smooth and without pauses is one way to keep the mind clear of distraction and allow improved ability to focus on the object of study, whatever that object of study might be.

When I first started to teach diaphragmatic breathing, I had people lie down on the floor and put their hands on their belly. Depending on their breath capacity, I would ask them to count from 1 to 4, or 1 to 6, during both inhalation and exhalation. I noticed that while students were breathing in this manner, the movement of the hand on the belly would slow or pause slightly with each count in their mind. Each time the content of the mind would change, the breath would fluctuate. For that reason, I began to ask students to simply focus on the smoothness of breath with or without the aid of a mantra that is meant to be combined with the breath (such as "soham").

XXXV. Letting the mind focus on the activity of the subtle senses can help establish steadiness of mind.

This and the following sūtra present the ability of the mind to achieve clarity by focusing on the subtle senses. By focusing on the subtle sense of touch, one can gain the ability to note the subtle kinesthetic sensations of the prāṇas.

Subtle sounds can also arise in certain areas of the body and lead one to focus on the subtle phenomena in an area of focus.

XXXVI. Also a serene or luminous state can lead to that clarity and steadiness of mind.

The subtle sense of vision can also lead consciousness in establishing clarity and steadiness of mind. As one practices meditation, fields of color appearing are not uncommon. They can help one intensify focus on a particular subtle region. As one begins to establish suṣumnā awareness, the fields of color can undergo change. For example, in a mystical state of suṣumnā awareness, they may organize themselves into a pattern of lotus petals which then opens from the center.

In some cases, a field of color appears to move closer to the observer. The meditator who has established suṣumnā awareness can then note that the field of color is not a solid field, but is actually a pattern of light in which there are spaces through which consciousness can pass. What has been veiled by the field of color then becomes visible. Visual perception of veils of color and nāḍis (energy pathways) are further described in the commentary of Sādhana Pāda, verse LII.

XXXVII. Clarity of mind can be gained by fixing the mind on those who are free from attachment.

An example of this would be to study and contemplate the life and actions of the great saints. On a more subtle level, one can bring the energy imprint of a great one into one's consciousness.

Something to consider:

What will you do and how will you choose to be when a great one visits you in your practice?

XXXVIII. Clarity of mind can also be gained by depending on knowledge derived from dream and dreamless sleep.

My teacher would say that when he appeared in a dream, it was not a dream. The masters sometimes teach us in our dreaming state of consciousness rather than in a waking state. My teacher would also say sometimes he could do his best work with us when we were asleep.

Patanjali may also have been referring to the state of yoga nidrā. In such a state, the practitioner maintains conscious awareness during the transitions into dream and deep sleep. If this can be achieved, much can be learned in this mystical state. The transitions between waking and dream state, or between dream state and deep sleep, are gateways to higher states of consiousness. The trick is to establish suṣumnā and not simply fall asleep in the normal manner during such transitions.

Practice: Yoga nidrā

There are many techniques taught in various traditions to lead the student toward the state of consciousness called yoga nidrā. Some common elements of many of these techniques are: 1) establish smoothness of breath; 2) try to establish free flow of prāṇa in all areas of the body; 3) clear the flow of prāṇa in the central channel; 4) balance the solar and lunar energies, the "ha" and the "tha"; 5) center the mind's tactile awareness in anāhata cakra while extending exhalation until it is twice as long as inhalation. Master these five steps without losing conscious awareness as the body goes into sleep state. This practice should be done with the final step lasting no more than ten minutes. The place of practice should be absolutely quiet with no chance of interruption as injury can occur if suddenly interrupted during this practice. The sense of sound is particularly acute and noise can damage the hearing mechanism.

The specific steps of yoga nidrā practice as originally taught to me are as follows:

1. Practice śavāsana with diaphragmatic breathing on a surface which allows for an erect spine. Practice should not be done in a soft bed such as a water bed, as this would allow the spine to curve instead of remaining erect. It is important that the lower rib cage not compress the abdomen while breathing. The neck should be supported as the supporting structures of the neck can become lax and strained with prolonged practice of śavāsana.

2. Preliminary practice is that of 61 points. This practice is used to survey the energy points and flows within the body. As the points are followed, establish a tactile awareness at each point. Rather than jumping from point-to-point, transition the

awareness tactiley through the tissues. For example, when allowing awareness to move from the shoulder to the elbow, try to feel the tissues of the biceps, triceps, humerus, and associated tendons. Move through the upper arm rather than jumping from the shoulder to the elbow. Make use of the subtle sense of touch to smooth the path of the prāṇas through the tissues.

Proceed through the points at a rate that ensures continuity of focus. As the practice deepens over time, there may be the appearance of points of light at each point of focus. There might also be a sense of actually being led through the practice rather than consciously directing the practice. One might also begin to identify the internal anatomy within oneself.

The accompanying table and diagram on the following two pages enumerate the points as they are to be followed.

Following the practice of 61 points, proceed to the practice of śīthalī karaṇa as described in step 3.

61 Points

Point	Focus	31	Heart Center
1	Between Eyebrows	32	Navel Center
2	Throat Center	33	Pelvic Region
3	Right Shoulder	34	Right Hip
4	Right Elbow	35	Right Knee
5	Right Wrist	36	Right Ankle
6	Tip of Right Thumb	37	Tip Right Big Toe
7	Tip Right Index F.	38	Tip Right 2nd Toe
8	Tip Right Middle F.	39	Tip Right 3rd Toe
9	Tip Right Ring F.	40	Tip Right 4th Toe
10	Tip Right Little F.	41	Tip Right 5th Toe
11	Right Wrist	42	Right Ankle
12	Right Elbow	43	Right Knee
13	Right Shoulder	44	Right Hip
14	Throat Center	45	Pelvic Region
15	Left Shoulder	46	Left Hip
16	Left Elbow	47	Left Knee
17	Left Wrist	48	Left Ankle
18	Tip of Left Thumb	49	Tip Left Big Toe
19	Tip Left Index F.	50	Tip Left 2nd Toe
20	Tip Left Middle F.	51	Tip Left 3rd Toe
21	Tip Left Ring F.	52	Tip Left 4th Toe
22	Tip Left Little F.	53	Tip Left 5th Toe
23	Left Wrist	54	Left Ankle
24	Left Elbow	55	Left Knee
25	Left Shoulder	56	Left Hip
26	Throat Center	57	Pelvic Region
27	Heart Center	58	Navel Center
28	Right Breast	59	Heart Center
29	Heart Center	60	Throat Center
30	Left Breast	61	Between Eyebrows

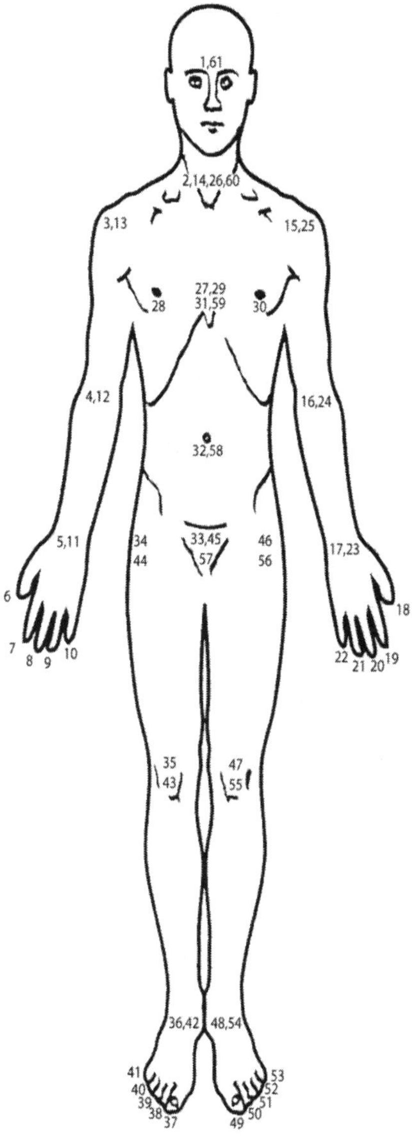
1,61
2,14,26,60
3,13
15,25
27,29
31,59
28
30
4,12
16,24
32,58
5,11
34
44
33,45
57
46
56
17,23
6
18
7
8
9
10
22
21
20
19
35
43
47
55
36,42
48,54
41
40
39
38
37
53
52
51
50
49

3. Śīthalī karaṇa is a practice to clear the prāṇa flow and the central channel between the cakras.

a. While exhaling downward and inhaling upward, follow the prāṇas between the following sets of points for ten breaths between each pair of points.

i. Crown of the head to the midpoint between the toes.

ii. Crown of the head to the midpoint between the ankles.

iii. Crown of the head to the midpoint between the knees.

b. Next exhale downward and inhale upward five times each between the cakras.

i. Sahasrāra and mūlādhāra cakras.

ii. Sahasrāra and maṇipūra cakras.

iii. Sahasrāra and anāhata cakras.

iv. Sahasrāra and viśuddha cakras.

v. Sahasrāra and ājñā cakras.

c. Focus on the prāṇa flow between the two nostrils (between the indentation above the upper lip through the nose bridge to ājñā cakra). As one exhales the prāṇa flow is downward and outward through that razor thin plane that separates the right and left. The flow is upward and inward on the inhale. Do this for at least ten breaths.

d. Repeat step (b) in the reverse order of pairing, still exhaling downward and inhaling upward with the prāṇa flow. Some practitioners also include the pairing between svādhiṣṭhāna and sahasrāra cakras in steps (b) and (d).

e. Repeat step (a) in reverse order.

f. Some practitioners simply prefer to feel the prāṇa flows between each pair of cakras while experiencing the resonance between each pair of cakras as well as between the energy points in step (a).

4. Lie on the left side and exhale and inhale ten times while focusing on the flow in the right nostril. Alternatively one can breathe as if the entire right side of the body is flowing with prāṇa.

5. Lie on the right side and exhale and inhale ten times while focusing on the flow in the left nostril. Alternatively one can breathe as if the entire left side of the body is flowing with prāṇa. The object of steps four and five is to get the nostrils to flow evenly if they are not already doing so. Alternatively one can remain supine and turn one's head to the side of the dominant nostril until the shift in dominance just begins to occur.

6. Lie on the back and begin exhaling and inhaling with the whole body. On the exhale apāṇa moves down the central channel and out laterally at each cakra and outward through every pore of the body. On the inhale the prāṇa moves inward laterally through every pore and cakra and then upward within the outer layer of the central channel.

7. Take three serene diaphragmatic breaths, merging the prāṇas and breath with soham at ājñā cakra.

8. By this time the central channel downward should be clearly in the mind's view. Bring the mind's focus to viśuddha cakra, and finally to anāhata cakra. Extend the exhalation to be longer than the inhalation until roughly a 2:1 ratio is reached. Keep the mind's focus within anāhata cakra.

XXXIX. Clarity of mind can also be obtained by means of meditation on anything that is uplifting.

This sūtra is a very general statement that meditation can lead to clarity of mind, provided that the object of focus is suitable for leading one to that clarity. If the student has difficulty selecting an object of meditation, the help of the teacher can be useful.

XL. Mastery of focus extends from the most minute particle of an atom to the greatest magnitude.

With mastery, the student can choose to meditate on anything that the student wishes to know.

XLI. The clear, or well polished mind in one whose modifications of mind have been weakened or almost annihilated, can have intuitive knowledge. In that state the cognizer (the knower), cognition (the process of knowing), and the cognized (the object of focus) are absorbed into one another.

Intuitive knowledge requires the temporary surrender of one's identity in order to allow consciousness to unite with the object of focus. The process of knowing then becomes experiencing the object of focus, as that object experiences itself. Our personality development in the process of life seeks to prepare us for the process of gaining intuitive knowledge.

The potential to discover and know who we are manifests in stages of personality growth. How do we develop our sense of self, of who we are? Psychological studies of ego development over the years can help to provide part of the answer to that question.

Once we are born, our sense of who we are is influenced by our experience of the world. The world seems to revolve around us and attend to us. On one level, caregivers respond to our cries and either meet or don't meet our every need. On a more subtle level, we dance to the rhythm of the world. If we slow down the motions of an infant on film, the child can be seen to be dancing in rhythm with the caregiver's voice with subtle motions responding in sync to every inflection and change in the caregiver's voice. As an infant, the world appears to revolve around us, and we, in turn, dance to the world's subtle rhythms.

Observe the joy an infant experiences with the close attention of a caregiver. Try mirroring the sounds, facial expressions, and gestures of a small child and observe the effect on that child. The child attends with great interest. Explore the environment of a child by letting the child lead with its interest. Mimic the child's behavior. If the child wants to put things in its mouth or play with a piece of fuzz on the rug, get down nose-to-nose with that child and put those same things in your mouth or play with that same fuzz on the rug. The child responds to that mirroring with positive attention.

Children who have such experiences with their caregivers develop a positive sense of themselves. Mirroring a child's behavior lets the child know that their behavior is good, and, hence, that they are good. They experience enough of an intuitive sense of goodness that they can feel positive even when later they begin to separate from their near constant desire for the caregiver's attention. They can begin to play out of sight or out of hearing of the caregiver and still feel positive, or secure in themselves. The longing to still feel connected to the caregiver is, in part, satisfied by the child's internal sense of being positive and secure.

As the child becomes a little older, around the ages of three to six, he/she begins to learn pretend games, becoming a monkey, a tree, or perhaps an airplane. The child recognizes separateness of his/her identity from objects of the world, yet maintains a sense of connectedness with these objects by pretending to be that object.

Still later, from around age 7 to near puberty, children learn to mimic their caregivers in speech and action, again recognizing separateness from the caregiver, yet retaining a desire to maintain an emotional sense of connectedness. The child wants to cook or paint like their caregiver. Children of this age tend to adopt the habits, language, and values of their caregivers.

In adolescence there is often some struggle to establish oneself autonomously in one's own separate identity. The desire to feel autonomous can conflict with the innate desire to feel connected. Power struggles can sometimes ensue with caregivers. During successful resolution of struggles with caregivers, an important development in personality can occur. A key personality development for successful negotiation and conflict resolution within families is the experience of empathy. The capacity for empathy allows one to experience the viewpoint of another human being, to be able to place oneself in another person's shoes and experience what that person feels and values. Successful negotiation and conflict resolution within families often depends on the ability to have empathy with other family members. The capacity for empathy allows a sense of connectedness to coexist while recognizing autonomy of decision making and reinforcing the apparent reality of separateness.

A goal of the mystical traditions of meditation is to become aware of, and be in harmony with, areas of knowledge previously inaccessible without mystical vision. How can we expect to be in harmony with the expanded knowledge available in the universe if we can't even be in harmony with the viewpoint and values of another human being? Empathy is an important step in developing intuitive knowledge, the ability to know by becoming that which we wish to understand. Intuitive knowledge allows us to witness separateness and connectedness simultaneously. In our internal exploration through meditation, intuitive knowledge allows us to experience ourselves as a diverse manifestation of the Creator while simultaneously knowing the diversity of manifestation of the Divine that has become ourselves.

To have intuitive knowledge, we have to surrender our sense of identity that makes us see ourselves as separate from that which we desire to know. We must instead merge our awareness with that which we wish to know, to consciously become the object of our study and experience the universe as our object of study experiences the universe. We allow ourselves to become similar to (tatstha) or take the color of (tadānjanatā) that which we seek to know in this state of samādhi or balanced state (samāpattiḥ).

Practice:

Take some time and pretend to be the Divine. Study how your mind handles this contemplation.

Something to consider:

Am I ready to be one with the Divine?

XLII. Savitarkā samādhi: mind alternates between ordinary knowledge based on sense perception and reasoning in the state of samādhi based on vitarka (application of the mind to that which is to be cognized).

The sense of self or I-am-ness is still intact.

XLIII. When the mind loses its essential nature (I-am-ness or ahaṃkāra), real knowledge of the object to be cognized shines. This is nirvitarkā samādhi.

XLIV. Samādhi by savicārā and nirvicārā has been explained.

This sūtra indicates that samādhi of subtle objects or the fine points of an object of study is similar to what has been previously described. For example, understanding the textures of the elements (earth, water, fire, air, ether) and their blend to become the object of study can also be understood in the state of samādhi with or without surrendering one's sense of I-am-ness.

XLV. The samādhi concerned with subtle objects extends to all things.

Part of the meaning of the sūtra concerns the ability to understand objects that are, as yet, not manifest. To understand this concept, it is important to understand the difference in the element that is sometimes translated as space, and at other times is translated as ether. Space has the quality of absolute emptiness. Ether, however, is that which occupies empty space that has yet to accept a vibration (spanda) in order to manifest as something. The quality, or texture, of ether is stillness until it accepts a vibration to actually become something.

XLVI. The aforementioned stages correspond to samādhi with "seed".

XLVII. With nirvicārā samādhi there is the dawning of spiritual light.

There is a difference in perceiving an object of the mind with the intellect versus perceiving it with the illumination of spiritual light accompanying the state of samādhi. Knowledge obtained with the dawning of spiritual light is clear and not corrupted by such influences as the refresh rate of the universe (the sequence of moments in time where the universe remerges and reappears many times per second).

XLVIII. After attaining that state one's consciousness attains knowledge that is truth-bearing or right-bearing (ṛtaṃbharā).

My teacher used to say that anyone who is to be the successor in his particular lineage of teachers (lineage of Bharati) had to have the ability to instantly know the answer to whatever question was posed. It is the state of nirvicārā samādhi that would allow one to have this ability. Being able to examine the question with illumination of the spiritual light gives that ability to instantly know the truth regarding the question posed.

XLIX. Knowledge based on inference and testimony is different than knowledge attained in higher states of consciousness.

L. In the state of sabīja samādhi, the impression in the mind produced by an object of focus stands in the way of other impressions which can no longer intrude.

When one has filled one's awareness with a particular content of mind in the conscious state of sabīja samādhi (samādhi with "seed"), no other content of mind can take the place of that particular "seed". This is an important concept to understand from the perspective of the tantric practices of transformation and transmutation. One must be able to even eliminate the void (the spaces between moments in time) from intruding upon one's awareness. The subject of transformation and transmutation will be dealt with in later sūtras.

LI. Suppression of all modifications of the mind allows for seedless samādhi (nirbīja samādhi).

When the energy of prāṇa attached to each impression in the mind has been attenuated, no saṃskāra pushes forward to occupy the content of the mind. Consciousness is then able to dwell without content of mind.

Sādhanā Pāda

I. Tapas, svādhyāya, and Īśvara-pranidhana constitute preliminary yoga.

Discipline, self-study, and surrender to the Divine are part of the preliminary practices of yoga. The literal translation of "tapas" is to burn or create heat. Tapas refers to burning impurities through self-discipline and yoga practice. "Kriyā" in reference to this and the following sūtras refers to preliminary or practical yoga.

II. Created this kriya practice to attenuate kleśas (obstacles or afflictions) to bring about samādhi.

III. The afflictions, or five kleśas, are: 1) lack of awareness, ignorance, or illusion; 2) I-am-ness, ego, ahaṃkāra; 3) attraction; 4) repulsion; 5) clinging to life or fear of death.

These afflictions are generally considered the causes of pain and misery. However, some of the afflictions are useful in our learning process of life. For example, the illusion of having an individual identity (ahaṃkāra) allows us to learn while focusing on a small portion of the universe instead of being aware of all the substance, issues, and imbalances of the universe at one time. If we were not blessed with this particular aspect of ignorance, it would be like trying to run a business by assigning every task of the entire business to one person. The person would be overwhelmed and nothing would be accomplished.

Attraction and repulsion both have the capacity to unsettle the mind. In everyday life, ordinary desires and aversions tend to influence the mind and command the energy of life. Both attraction and repulsion can lead one off the path of yoga, interfering with the pursuit of that knowledge to be gained by that conscious state called samādhi.

Lack of knowledge of what consciousness was before life, or what will become of consciousness after death of the body, can both contribute to the fear of death. If we are in a well lit room and we are familiar with all the objects and circumstance within the room, there is little fear of the unknown. If, however, we are asked to open the door labeled "death," and what we see through the doorway is absolute darkness with no floor, walls or ceiling visible, there is some hesitancy about stepping through that doorway. The path of yoga seeks to provide illumination even beyond that doorway marked "death".

Practice:

Contemplate the conscious experience you will have after your death.

Something to consider:

What do you wish to do, or how do you wish to be before the time of death? When the time comes, with what state of awareness do you wish to experience the transition of consciousness called death?

IV. Avidyā (lack of knowledge) is the basic source of the afflictions. These afflictions can either be dormant, feeble or attenuated, intercepted (scattered, dispersed, alternating), or sustained and expanded (fully operating).

In a baby the kleśas are generally considered to be dormant. Once the goal of yoga is reached, they might also be considered to be dormant. Along the path of yoga kleśas can be attenuated through the practices which influence the mind. For example, the practice of kevala kumbhaka can help attenuate the fear of death by voluntarily experiencing the union of prāṇa and apāṇa with suspension of the need to breathe for an extended period of time. A near-death experience might also attenuate the fear of death.

For many, the kleśas are sustained and fully operating in day-to-day life.

Something to consider:

How would you lead life differently if you truly believed consciousness to be eternal instead of impermanent?

V. Avidyā is taking the non-eternal (impermanent), impure, evil, and non-Ātman to be eternal, pure, good, and Ātman.

Ātman refers to that divine spark before it is surrounded by her layers of ignorance and burdened by karmas to become an individual soul.

An example of ignorance would be the attempts by human cultures over the ages to assign characteristics, wishes, and names to the Divine. This habit has led to wars, prejudices, and cruelties that have fostered great misery for humanity over the centuries.

VI. Asmitā is the identity that is the blending together of the power of consciousness (Puruṣa) with the power of cognition or knowing.

An aspect of asmitā includes identification of our mind with the product of the senses. For example, we see our reflection in the mirror and consider it to be ourselves. We hear the sound of our speech, and consider the words to be ours.

When we have thoughts and feelings, we own them and consider them to be ours. We consider them to be products of our own mind. We consider ourselves to have roles in life, such as husband, wife, parent, child, worker, boss, etc.

Our sense of I-am-ness or ego (ahaṃkāra) is a reflection of our true Self, yet in our ignorance of our true Self, we identify ourselves as the reflection.

VII. Rāgaḥ: that attraction which accompanies pleasure.

The seeking of pleasure can be considered a substitute for the connection lost within ourselves. Just as a child seeks the presence of a caregiver, humanity throughout the ages has sought to feel in the presence of the Creator. Many substitutes for the goal of connectedness result in temporary pleasures. We run here and there with our minds becoming desirous of and attached to objects of pleasure in our ignorance that the bliss and presence of the Divine is already within us.

Something to consider:

What if you are the entire universe and it is only the limits of your consciousness that keeps you from realizing this?

VIII. Dveṣaḥ: that repulsion that accompanies pain.

Dveṣaḥ and rāgaḥ are both considered obstacles on the path of yoga. Both dveṣaḥ and rāgaḥ are examples of unsteadiness of mind. At times one can experience rāgaḥ and dveṣaḥ toward the same object. For example, if one sees a particular car, desires that car, pictures oneself driving that car, and yet can't afford to buy that car, attraction and repulsion can occur simultaneously toward the car.

IX. Abhiniveśa, the strong desire for life is sustained by its own potency or inherent force even in the wise, as it is a result from past habit as well as fear of what lies ahead.

One December evening at the Himalayan Institute in Honesdale, Pennsylvania, my teacher was to lead a kirtan during a conference entitled "The Path of Fire and Light". As I was sitting in the auditorium preparing myself for the kirtan prior to my teacher's arrival, I realized I had not picked up the word sheet that listed the phrases for the particular chants. I quickly rose from my seat and moved speedily to the closed double doors at the back of the auditorium. As I burst through the doors I nearly collided with my teacher as he was about to enter the auditorium. I quickly grabbed a word sheet and returned to my seat. As my teacher sat down I noted that I had picked a place directly in line with the middle of his torso.

The usual routine for the kirtan was to do several chants of ten minutes or so each, after which the evening prayers were recited before people filed off to their rooms. As the chanting progressed, I noted that my breathing was changing into a very full, perfectly smooth, diaphragmatic breath. Towards the end of each inhalation, I noted a sense of bliss beginning to emerge. At the beginning of one of the chants and at the end of a blissful inhalation, I ceased to breathe. What followed was what many would call śaktipāta, complete with an experience of Divine Mother raising that central energy within me. My perception in that state of kevala kumbhaka was that a few minutes had passed. A thought arose in my mind, "Isn't it time to breathe?" When I opened my eyes, the chanting had apparently finished, the evening prayers had apparently already been performed, and there were only two other people left in the auditorium, one of whom was still meditating, and the other of whom was fast asleep against the wall of the auditorium.

Despite having had this experience of kevala kumbhaka and a prior experience in life of a near-death experience (drowning as a child), I was not ready to accept the offer of an experience of nirbīja samādhi later in life. I still had attachments to my responsibilities in life that I feared I could not fulfill if I were to give up my identity and merge with the Divine in the abode of Divine Mother. I still had a fear that death would result in an incompleteness of life. I did not yet trust that I would be okay if I died or permanently gave up my current conscious identity.

X. The obstacles can be resolved by reducing or resolving them backward into their origins.

The origin of the obstacles or afflictions is thought to be the ego and its lack of memory regarding the origins of one's particular identity in a current life. This is thought to be the origin of fears regarding that loss of identity.

XI. Active modifications of the mind (such as desires, aversions, or fears) are suppressed by meditation.

Obstacles such as desires, aversions, and fears have energy and feelings attached to them. It is the energy and feelings which allow the obstacles to keep pushing forward to occupy the mind's attention. The practice of meditation seeks to diminish the potency of such obstacles. Mediation seeks to reduce the prāṇa and affect attached to those impressions of the mind (saṃskāras) that are most involved in the creation of the desires, aversions, and fears.

The practice of meditation eventually seeks to quiet all modifications of the mind, and not merely more noticeable obstacles. One needs to understand the process of meditation as well as the goal of meditation in order to fully comprehend how such a goal might be achieved. Techniques of meditation most often involve attempting to keep the mind focused on a single content, such as a mantra, yantra, or other object of focus. Because of saṃskāras, there is pressure exerted upon one's conscious mind to change the mind's focus. While meditating on the mantra, the mind might give the meditator the message "I'm hungry." The thought of having some ice cream might then come into the mind. The following diagram illustrates this.

A̲ x A̲ x B̲ x A̲ x A̲ x C̲ x A̲

A̲ = mantra

B̲ = "I'm hungry."

C̲ = thought of having some ice cream

x = break between thoughts

When one achieves perfect concentration (dhāraṇā) there can still be breaks between the thoughts or contents of mind, but the content of mind will be exactly the same except for the breaks. The following diagram illustrates perfect concentration.

A̲ x A̲ x A̲ x A̲ x A̲ x A̲ x A̲

A̲ = mantra

x = break between thoughts

Both attempting to achieve perfect concentration, as well as the achievement of perfect concentration are intermediate steps to reaching the goal of meditation (dhyāna). Regardless of the technique employed, the goal of meditation is to achieve unbroken focus of the mind upon a single content of mind. Even the spaces between the thoughts are eliminated. The following diagram illustrates.

A------------------------------------→

The goal of meditation illustrated above results in the state of bliss capable of reducing the meditator's attachment to any other content of mind.

The meaning of this sūtra is twofold. Modifications of the mind (the intrusive effect of saṃskāras) can be eliminated both by the techniques of meditation, as well as by the goal of achieving meditation. The modifications of the mind involving the blank spaces between the thoughts, however, require the goal of meditation to be realized. The nature of these blank spaces between contents of mind will be further discussed in section four (Kaivalya Pada) of the Yoga Sūtras.

XII. Karmas are rooted in the kleśas. The fruits of our actions in thought, speech, and deed are reaped in both present and future lives.

Every thought of our mind, every word of our speech, every action performed by us carry an energy and vibration that registers in both the individual mind as well as the collective mind. If our actions, thoughts, and speech are influenced by misapprehension of reality, such that there is an erroneous identification of who we actually are (māyā), then this misapprehension results in karmic consequences. Māyā is that illusion that we are individual, or separate from the Divine. Māyā is that erroneous identification of who we are, having us think that we are our own individual intellect. This misapprehension as well as associated attractions, aversions, or fears, leads to invoking the law of karma. The law of karma states that we will have to reap the fruits of actions, thoughts, and words spoken.

Something to consider:

When there is no misapprehension of reality, realization of the true Self, can there be any karma resulting from actions, thoughts, and speech?

XIII. As long as the roots in the aforementioned kleśas are there, the karmic fruits ripen and result in lives of different class, length, and experiences (pleasant and unpleasant).

A mind is created through the union of two aspects of the Divine. One aspect of the Divine is the potential to become all that exists. This potential is given different names by different traditions. Some of the names are Śiva, God the Father, or Holy Father. Another aspect of the Divine is the power of creation. This power also has various names such as Śakti, Divine Mother, kuṇḍalinī, and Holy Spirit. The union of divine potential and the force of creation must proceed through whatever layers of ignorance are still present at the time of the mind's creation. Forming part of the layers of ignorance through which creation passes are the karmas that continue to influence the creation of the mind. The karmas help to determine what sort of obstacles and opportunities one will face in life. Those obstacles and opportunities, in part, might be expressed in one's birth circumstance. They may also help determine how long one might live. The persistence of a past habit of desiring smoking tobacco, for example, might shorten one's current life.

Something to consider:

If one has complete knowledge and no further need to learn anything, does one need to be born to face any opportunities or obstacles in life?

XIV. Joy or sorrow from the fruits of karma are according to their cause, whether virtue or vice (merits or demerits).

XV. For those who have developed discrimination, all is misery on account of: 1) pain resulting from change, anxiety, and tendencies; 2) conflicts between the functioning of the guṇas and the vṛttis.

Past experience can give rise to desires and aversions. If one stays attached to those desires and aversions instead of being detached and content with the process of life, pain is the result. As an alternative, one can accept the world as our collective unconscious, a collection of all the opportunities and obstacles we need to learn from both individually and collectively. One can then detach from the desires and miseries and succeed in the goal of mastering oneself in the process of a life that has been gifted through the process of creation.

In this sūtra, the vṛittis refer to the whirling of the mind that attempts to make sense of that which is presented to the mind. What is presented to the mind for its analysis and interpretation arises from the three tendencies (guṇas) and their interplay with Prakṛiti (universal nature). The three tendencies are sattva guṇa, rajas guṇa, and tamas guṇa. Sattva guṇa refers to the tendency toward purity, clarity, lucidity, or existence with a quality of balance or order. Rajas guṇa refers to movement, dynamism, or change. Tamas guṇa refers to the tendency to preserve sameness and also is sometimes thought of as the tendency toward resistance to (inertia) or destruction of the process of change. When the mind's analysis of what is presented for interpretation is not accurate, particularly regarding the false perception of reality, pain is the result.

XVI. The misery that is not yet come can and is to be avoided.

One of the goals of yoga is to avoid the pain caused by ignorance. The actions resulting from such ignorance have the potential to cause painful fruits of karma.

XVII. The cause of that misery to be avoided is the union of the seer and the seen.

In our ignorance, we tend to identify with our bodies, our thoughts and feelings, and our prāṇas. We then see ourselves as individuals rather than as that divine spark from which we came. We look in the mirror and think we are looking at ourselves. We have feelings, and think they belong only to us rather than having potential influence outside of ourselves. We think we are alone because we do not see someone else in the room. We learn to feel flows of our prāṇas and think they belong to us rather than extending the perception of those prāṇas to the entire universe. This limited view of ourselves is a source of misery, particularly when we try to answer the questions of who we are, from where did we come, and where are we going after this life.

XVIII. The seen (elements and sense organs) is of the nature of sattva, rajas, and tamas. The purpose of the phenomenal world is to provide experience and liberation.

The elements referred to in this sūtra refer to the elements of earth, water, fire, air, and ether (also translated as space). In Sanskrit these are known as the bhūtas, that which is the makeup of everything created in the world. There is a difference between the concept of space and the concept of ether. Space is emptiness. Ether is that potential which occupies space that has not yet accepted a vibration or texture in order to become something. When the ether in a particular space accepts a vibration, it becomes an admixture of the textures and properties of the elements of earth, water, fire, and air. The tendencies of the guṇas are involved in the interplay of the elements that become the gross and subtle objects of the world. This admixture is what is then seen through the perception of one's sense organs. The sight, taste, scent, feel, and sound of biting into a slice of orange or a slice of apple will differ because the admixture of the elements that make up a slice of the orange or the slice of the apple are different.

The second part of this sūtra describes the reason for the existence of the phenomenal world as being to provide the opportunities and obstacles from which we need to learn. Some commentators interpret liberation as the liberation of the individual from ignorance, allowing the individual to then merge in awareness with the Divine.

Something to consider:

If we are all contained within each other, and it is only our ignorance that allows us to see ourselves as separate, then the concept of liberation takes on an entirely different meaning. Liberation refers to our no longer collectively needing to have the phenomenal world provide us with opportunities and obstacles for growth. This is presumably because we would have collectively found the knowledge that allowed us to move to the next step in our evolution. What will be the state of the world before the next step in our collective evolution?

XIX. The stages of the guṇas are fourfold: specific, non-specific, defined, and indefinable.

Viśeṣa means the mind sees objects as particular or specific things. Viśeṣa can be translated as particular. This involves an activity of the mind called vitarka, which is an activity of the mind that differentiates a particular object from all other particular objects. The mind might interpret an object as being an apple as opposed to an orange, for example.

Aviśeṣa means universal or non-specific, such as the mind seeing universal archetypes and principles. An activity of the mind, vicāra, allows us to see more subtle aspects of a particular object upon which the mind is focused. For example, if we smell the fragrance of an orange that has been freshly cut, we might still associate that fragrance with the concept of an orange. On a still more subtle level, one can sense energetics, the prāṇas, or auras of a particular object.

Liṅga – mātra is the state of consciousness where objects or principles are only marks or signs for the mind. Liṅga - mātra is an identifier to distinguish the object or principles from other objects or principles. The orange or apple is seen as a product of creation called fruit. Despite these marks or signs that help to distinguish objects (impressions in the mind) from one another, there is recognition that everything is seen as being embedded in the universe as a whole.

Āliṅga means indefinable, without differentiation or characteristics. In āliṅga stage of the guṇas, the mind is aware of the Divine that permeates all objects and principles. The guṇas are in the state of perfect equilibrium. That subtle element of ether which has not yet accepted a vibration or tendency to become something would be āliṅga.

XX. Pure consciousness (Puruṣa) sees through the content of the mind.

As we become aware of our true nature, we can recognize the illusion of the universe that is a product of our collective and individual ignorance. When we gain the perspective of pure consciousness, the world we live in is recognized as a manifestation capable of teaching us. In order to truly understand that aspect of ourselves that is capable of creating the world, we must experience that process of creation. The illusion of our becoming manifest as separate from one another through the process of creation is part of our education process.

XXI. Prakṛiti (the manifest) exists only for Puruṣa (the unmanifest or undifferentiated).

The manifest world exists only for our education and growth, and for no other purpose. Puruṣa is considered that aspect of ourselves that is divine potential prior to manifest-tation or differentiation into the individuals that we ordinarily perceive ourselves to be.

Practice:

Contemplate all that you experience as being a divine gift.

XXII. Prakṛiti continues to exist for others, even though one may have reached the goal of yoga.

Māyā, the illusion of creation, appears real for those who have not yet understood the world to be a manifestation of ourselves. For one who has attained the goal of yoga, which is awareness of the union of body, mind, and spirit with the Divine, māyā is then recognized and understood. The union of body, mind, and spirit with the Divine can also be understood as the union of Prakṛiti and Puruṣa.

Practices:

1. Love thy neighbor (or family member or co-worker) as thyself.

2. Treat yourself at least as well as you would treat others.

XXIII. The purpose of the union of Puruṣa and Prakṛiti is to understand Puruṣa's true nature and the unfoldment of the powers (potential for manifestation) inherent in Him and Prakṛiti.

Without manifestation we cannot understand our true Self. The capacity to unite our consciousness with the force of manifestation cannot be understood without expression of the principle of manifestation and the conscious experience of becoming manifest. We have to consciously experience our own conception and creation of our self. Part of the education of the yogi or yogini is to witness the union of divine potential and force of manifestation as a conscious experience, and then to experience the result of that union as something created.

XXIV. The cause of the union of Prakṛiti and Puruṣa is lack of awareness of one's true nature.

It is because of the ignorance of the reality of who we are that the manifestation of this universe, and of this world, is necessary. A product of creation that we are familiar with in the ordinary sense, is the conception of children and the manifestation of that conception through the birth of a child. Few, however, experience the energetic union of divine potential and force of manifestation that led to the conception of that child and the soul embedded within that child. Fewer still, consciously remember the energetic events of their own conception, or their own death.

In observation of natural phenomena, we are given a glimpse of the process of creation. We understand that lightning in nature first creates a silent void, a physical vacuum. We then understand the rush to fill that space or void sets up a vibration that we experience audibly as thunder. If we are close enough, we might also experience with our tactile senses the trembling of the earth and the concussion of the thunder. This natural event bears some resemblance to the revelation of a mantra to a seer. If one enters a state of samādhi and proceeds to an area of consciousness called the ocean of beauty, one might witness the union of a single aspect of divine potential with the force of creation (Śiva and Śakti). This union resembles lightning in that what is first created is a profound silence. The rush to fill that silence sets up a vibration that can become a mantra or yantra revealed.

XXV. Elimination of avidyā is the means to liberation of the seer.

Avidyā, or lack of knowledge, is considered the cause of non-union of Prakṛiti and Puruṣa. Once the yogi/yogini recognizes their true Self, they become independent in terms of their need for this world to teach them something. As ones who have tread the path already, however, those liberated from the need to be born may still choose to be active in the world in the service of others who have not yet attained that liberation. The liberated ones may be active as manifest or unmanifest beings.

XXVI. Uninterrupted awareness of the real is the means of eliminating avidyā.

The means of eliminating lack of knowledge (avidyā) involves vivek-khyātiḥ, knowledge of discrimination of the real from the unreal. To experience the union of body, mind, and spirit with the Divine one must be able to distinguish the real from the unreal.

XXVII. There are seven stages to the highest state of enlightenment. Signs of progress are the absence of desires and attractions, aversions, the desire to gain anything new, the desire to do anything, as well as the absence of sorrow, fear, and delusion.

In the first stage we come to know that pursuing knowledge externally or deductively does not accomplish the goal of uniting body, mind, and spirit with the Divine. In the second stage we recognize that pleasure and pain are products of the mind and are not determined by external circumstance. In the third stage we have a neutral mind, recognizing that all knowledge can be gained from experiencing the true Self. In the fourth stage we recognize that there is no desire to do any particular thing, understanding that the natural world is merely a cosmic play. One can choose to participate in that cosmic play, particularly in regards to that which is of service and is helpful in the world, but there is no attachment to one's actions.

Something to consider:

What would you do in the world if you were free of desires and aversions?

In the fifth stage the mind is free of impressions that have affect such as fear, sorrow, or desire attached. Prāṇa no longer remains attached to impressions. There is no energy to have those impressions or saṃskāras continue to press forward to create a wave or disturbance in the mind.

In the sixth stage the mind itself is dissolved as no longer being necessary for the perception of the real. In the seventh stage is the union of consciousness with the Divine Self and understanding of that Self.

XXVIII. Spiritual illumination and destruction of impurities comes from the practice of components of yoga.

Here "yoga" refers to kriya yoga, the preliminary practices before the goal of yoga is attained.

XXIX. The eight limbs of yoga are yama, niyama, āsana, prāṇāyāma, pratyāhāra, dhāraṇā, dhyāna, and samādhi.

These limbs are generally translated as attitudes and observances (yamas and niyamas), postures (āsanas), regulation or restraint of the prāṇas (prāṇāyāma), sense withdrawal (pratyāhāra), concentration (dhāranā), meditation (dhyāna), and expansion of consciousness (samādhi).

XXX. The yamas are abstaining from violence, falsehood, theft, attachment to sensual pleasures, and acquisitiveness.

Every word, thought, and action carries a vibration of energy that can allow it to affect us on a conscious or unconscious level. Dreams are a mobilization of this energy connected with past impressions, as are thoughts with enough energy to enter our awareness despite our resolve to meditate. The following yamas help to reduce the pressures within the mind that obstruct or disturb clarity while pursuing the path of yoga.

Nonviolence: Ahiṃsā is defined as non-harming or non-violence. It has many practical aspects. Being at peace with all our decisions and actions is necessary to allow consciousness to proceed untroubled in the exploration of self. Part of the training in all the mystical traditions that I am familiar with is the principle of nonviolence in thought, word, and speech. A sense of nonviolence is considered necessary to proceed with decisions and actions without internal conflict or karmic repercussions, both of which can distract the practitioner from exploration of self.

What does nonviolence look like on a practical level? If a child is about to insert a paper clip into an electrical outlet, what does one do? The first thing one might do is yell at the child with sufficient alarm and/or anger to immediately stop the child from electrocuting him or herself. After the initial display of emotion for behavioral effect, one can then teach the child more gently about both the benefits and dangers of electricity. The idea of measuring one's emotional response to fit the situation in a way that teaches rather than harms is important in mastering the principle of nonviolence.

How does one respond to the violent actions or intent of others? The message of the Bhagavad Gita and other scriptures is quite clear on this. Do battle when it is a necessary response to the actions of others, but do not develop an attachment to enjoying the process of war. It is a skill to keep peace in the heart while at the same time acting to keep peace in the land or in the home. Atrocities during wartime, in law enforcement, and in domestic settings are common when peace in the heart is not maintained during the performance of one's duties in life. It is a skill to measure one's response to violent intent. Highly skilled practitioners of the martial arts are also known for their steadiness of mind. There are numerous examples in history where attempting to control a nation through violence and oppression has only led to revolution. Mutually satisfying relationships between human beings are not based on violent intent.

Something to consider:

Swallowing emotions such as anger in the face of confrontation can be just as much a poison for the mind as doing violence toward others. Such emotional suppression is a form of violence toward oneself. Many physical ailments are thought to have emotional suppression as a factor creating or influencing the ailment.

Keeping peace in one's heart regardless of external circumstance is a skill worth mastering. It is part of the development of object constancy, that psychological concept that allows one to maintain equanimity in the face of challenge and change. A challenge we all face is the challenge of death, all too often perceived as something to be feared or dreaded. Some perceive death as an act of violence done by the world against them. Approaching death with equanimity is a challenge to our sense of object constancy. Life is the training ground to develop that equanimity to handle such transitions.

Truthfulness: The practice of truthfulness (satya) and honesty has many benefits for the yoga practitioner. The practice of being truthful is part of many mystical traditions. The process of cultivating truthfulness is said by the mystics to be part of what allows the mind to shine with such brilliance that only truth can be perceived. Lying to others makes us more likely to doubt the truth spoken or authored by others. Doubt can also arise regarding trusting the validity of observation of our internal experiences. If we cannot act truthfully in life, how can we see the truth within? A willingness to be truthful tends to become second nature for those on a quest of their inner frontier.

A place to start the practice of truthfulness on the path of yoga is to be honest with ourselves. Being true to ourselves in the choices we make in life is important on our spiritual journey. It helps in finding a balance with our roles in the world. Violating our conscience with the choices we make in life is one form of not being honest with ourselves. For example, resenting our jobs or our relationships with others is not helpful for a mind trying to follow the path of meditation. Those resentments registering repeatedly in our minds tend to push thoughts and feelings based on these resentments forward into our awareness during times when we are trying to practice our meditation. Resentments can also unbalance us medically with stress related disorders and, in so doing, further distract us from our spiritual practice.

How does one not kill the conscience while performing one's duties in the world? "Grease all you do with love." my teacher would say. From a spiritual perspective, an attitude of peace and love in your heart while performing your duties in the world is more important than what those actual duties are. An area of stress for many is the stress of a job one does not enjoy. How does one grease what you do with love in a job you dislike? If you have a job that does not agree with you, at least understand the practical and emotional reasons of why you are there. What does this job do for you? What does this job do for others? Why do you resent the job? What is the belief that facilitates that resentment? Is that belief valid? What would the job feel like if you did not hold that belief? Is there another job that would be practical for you and be more in harmony with your beliefs and wishes? If so, how will you put yourself in a position to do that job? How would you practically pursue your dreams in life without your current job? Make a plan either for a change in your attitude about the current job, or for a change that will still accomplish the practical goals met by the current job and allow you to earnestly pursue your dreams.

Another example of not practicing truthfulness on the path of life is when we are not honest with ourselves in relationships. When a relationship in life feels difficult, first seek to understand the difficulty. Be honest about it. A relationship is made up of at least two people, including you. Try to understand the feelings, emotions, and viewpoints of all involved. Remember that empathy is a training ground for learning to merge your awareness with an object of focus to understand from an intuitive perspective rather than from a deductive analysis. It is sometimes helpful to contemplate your feelings and thoughts, your faults and strengths, your errors and right actions before attempting to put yourself in another person's shoes and contemplate their involvement and viewpoint. Be honest with yourself and you will be better able to honestly assess others.

A useful book to study regarding finding peace in the heart in relationships and in life is Love Is The Answer by Jerald Jampolski and Diane Cirincioni. This book is a simple to read, shortened version of a larger text, A Course In Miracles by the Foundation For Inner Peace. It contains many practical tips and exercises to begin the journey of finding peace in the heart with one's role in the world. If we kill our conscience every day in our actions of life, can we enter our internal frontier with equanimity?

Honest observation of ourselves in making major decisions in life is also part of the path of truthfulness. Major decisions in life can facilitate or hinder us on the path of yoga. Some decisions are made primarily on an emotional basis with the feelings in one's heart. This is frequently the basis in relationship choices. Other decisions are made primarily with the cognitive input of the mind. For important decisions in life it is usually best to have the heart and mind both agree before taking action or making choices. If they don't agree, it may be best to examine why the disagreement is there before taking action or making the choice.

How many people fall in love and choose a partner in life only to have it fall apart or feel bad at a later time? Unfortunately, this scenario is all too common. Many years ago, when it came time for my wife to choose a partner, she received some very wise advice. "Make a list," her friend told her, "and underline or star the things you won't compromise on." Take some time to make such a list, and then don't forget to use the list when you meet someone and your chemistry and emotions say "Wow!" Whether it be decisions about a job, a relationship, a place to live, or any other important decision, the mind's honest assessment of the factors involved may be just as important as feelings in the heart.

Non-stealing: Non-stealing (asteya) is also an important restraint on the spiritual path. What kind of a world would we live in if the business and political leaders of the world adopted the attitude of attending to only those ideas that would help others in addition to helping themselves? Would you vote for a political candidate campaigning on the following platform? "If you have an idea that helps others in addition to helping yourself, come see me. If you have an idea or program that seeks to help yourself by depriving or taking away from others, please knock on the other candidates' doors."

If such win-win attitudes would be desirable in business and political leaders, why do we not adopt them for ourselves in the context of our own relationships in life? Taking away from someone for personal benefit is an indication of attachment to things of the external world. Focusing too intently on the external diverts the mind from internal observation. Not coveting (thought of stealing) and not stealing (action) help us to live in harmony with others. On the path of yoga our awareness expands to include all. If we cannot learn to live in harmony with a few others, how can we be in harmony with ourselves when that expansion of awareness occurs to include all?

Something to consider:

What would the world be like without jealousy and greed?

Brahmacarya: Brahmacarya is frequently translated as celibacy, chastity, or sexual continence. A more literal translation is walking the path of Brahman. In the Vedic traditions brahmacarya is also considered a phase of life that can lead one toward knowledge of Brahman. The path of Brahman is more than mere celibacy. Walking the path of Brahman involves being unattached to the sensual pleasures of the world. If pleasant tasting, healthy food is offered to you when you are hungry, do you refuse food because it is tasty? Not keeping the body nourished is unhealthy, and poor health can distract you from the goal of yoga. You can learn to enjoy the sensual pleasures of the world without craving them. The practice of brahmacarya might take the form of enjoying the taste of a wonderful dessert offered, but not making a habit of having that dessert with every meal.

During some of my early trips to India, a morning meal of tasteless gruel was often the habit at ashrams. Many people are not constitutionally suited to eat a diet that tastes like cardboard. Enjoy the tastes offered, but make certain your overall diet nourishes you and helps you achieve your goals of life. Diet can help you enhance your health and your focus for meditative experience, or it can undermine your health and your practice. Please learn to discriminate what tasteful food choices are most helpful to you. This may involve exploring your ayurvedic constitution and experimenting with food choices that are both satisfying and constitutionally balancing. Find a balanced diet that the mind and senses can both enjoy or the subtle conflicts of denial will register in the unconscious and push forward to disturb the mind.

If your body needs shelter, do you refuse to put a roof over your head? Walking the path of Brahman means being able to make oneself at home in any dwelling when shelter is needed, whether the dwelling be modest or majestic.

If one has a partner in life, sexual abstinence might be harmful to the relationship and distract one from pursuing a spiritual path. One practice of brahmacarya during relations with your partner might be making your goal to facilitate your partner's pleasure rather than focusing on your own sensations. This is an exercise in non-attachment. Another practice of brahmacarya is to focus on the prāṇas around the heart center during sexual activity and recall the times of appreciation and delight in your relationship with your partner rather than being preoccupied with the sexual sensations. While sexual response may be slowed by this practice, the emotional satisfaction of the encounter can be blissful.

Attending to the prāṇas at the lower cakras can also provide insight regarding the relationship of the prāṇas to those centers as well as enhancing enjoyment of the experience of sexual expression. Walking the path of Brahman does not mean celibacy. It means not being attached to whether one indulges sexually or not for one's own pleasure.

For the yoga practitioner, pleasurable experiences in the world are no longer an impediment on the spiritual path as long as the practitioner does not remain attached to the seeking of pleasures.

Non-acquisitiveness: Aparigraha, non-acquisitiveness, is also part of the disciplines of many spiritual traditions. We have choices in life. We can acquire possessions as tools for service in the world without attachment. Alternatively, we can become attached to the process of acquiring, never feeling that what we have is enough. These are choices in how one relates to possessions.

My teacher's advice was "make use of and enjoy the things of the world, but do not become attached to them." Mother Theresa frequently identified the principal source of poverty and misery in the world as "we human beings." The desire to acquire for oneself at the expense of others is an example of acquisitiveness.

There is a time in life to be less concerned with accumulation of knowledge and material wealth, and to be more focused on sharing and service. Someone looking at their possessions to judge the worth of their life all too often feels the emptiness at the end of life when it is time to leave those possessions behind.

XXXI. Class or station in life, birth circumstance, place or location, setting in time, current circumstance, or any other factors do not modify the Great Vow.

The vows of restraint of the previous sūtras (the yamas) apply to all who wish to pursue the path of yoga.

XXXII. Observances (niyamas) are purity, contentment, austerity, self-study, and self-surrender.

Purity: Purity (śauca) can take many forms. Śauca in the niyamas does not denote physical or moral purity in the usual sense, though can lead to those forms of purity. Śauca embodies the quality of clarity. Purity of mind and body leads to the cultivation of mindfulness (smṛti) and discrimination (buddhi). As described previously, the discriminative level of the mind is developed to differentiate in our awareness that which fluctuates and changes (mind, body, breath, and prāṇa) from that which has no need to change (the source of ourselves). The discriminative level of the mind also helps us discern that which is helpful for the development of purity and that which clouds that purity of mind.

Remember that the mind, however, is also influenced by body and prāṇa. Also remember that the mind has both a conscious and an unconscious component. Since the body influences the mind, one must decide what is helpful or harmful to the body. Balancing the body and its bio-chemistry is part of balancing the mind. Nutritional decisions, lifestyle decisions, choices about medications or substances used, all affect purity of mind and body. The general rule is to do what is helpful in achieving balance and avoid what is not helpful.

Certain emotions can get in the way of purity of mind. We have looked at attachments, nonviolence, and other attitudes of mind in the yamas. One emotion that often plagues people's minds for lengthy times is that of guilt. Guilt and shame are often obstacles to emotional balance. My teacher would say "Learn from mistakes in order not to repeat them."

Practice regarding grief and shame:

No one goes through life without making mistakes. Consider that mistakes are part of the learning process of life. My teacher would say to learn from the mistake, examine the guilt associated with the mistake, and then offer that guilt to the divine fire within. That divine fire is sometimes visualized as residing at the navel center, the heart center, or the space between the eyebrows. As one offers the guilt to the flame, one consciously lets go of the energy of the mind connected to that guilt and experiences self-forgiveness.

Something to consider:

Accompanying the feelings of shame at times is the thought that we are somehow not normal. In my psychiatry training residency, I sat for a time to contemplate the idea of "normal" as compared to "abnormal," as those terms appeared repeatedly in the readings and discussions about diagnosis and behaviors. During that contemplation I concluded "normal" people don't have to be born. There is nothing here in life for them to do or work on. Consider that being abnormal is part of the design of life that allows us to learn what we need to know.

Practice regarding fears:

Fear is another emotion that can be an obstacle to progress. It is an interesting emotion in that it serves to protect us and help us survive on one level, but also can cloud our mind, particularly in the case of repetitive fears without obvious cause. One can practice relaxation techniques to manage the physiological component of fear, but repetitive fears can become a habit if more is not done. One can explore cognitively the issues relating to the fears through counseling, discussions, and the like.

An exercise one can do with one's own mind around such unexplained fears is to try to discern any belief that is behind that fear. If a belief is found, contemplate how one would lead life or deal with an aspect of life without that belief or that fear. Then resolve and choose how to be with that knowledge.

Fear of failure also can complicate our thinking. As my teacher used to say, "There is no such thing as failure, only loss of time." The guiding principle of love underlying this universe certainly offers us other opportunities to learn a lesson we had difficulty learning the first time. This principle may not always feel like love when the opportunity is offered, as life opportunities sometimes use pain to get our attention. However, if we look past the pain, there can be recognition that we are not being forsaken forever, but that we are simply being given another opportunity to learn. As my wife says from time to time, "Divine Mother put a stick of dynamite in your life." It is my task to learn from the explosion, not to forever bemoan its effects.

Contentment: Contentment (saṃtoṣa) is key to achieving balance in emotional life. Contentment is closely related to self-surrender (Īśvara praṇidhāna). If one has not mastered contentment, one cannot surrender one's ego when it is time to join with the consciousness of the Divine. Contentment involves feeling secure in the moment. The sense of security is related to a psychological construct called object constancy, where one has the sense that one is okay no matter the circumstance of the moment or the circumstance of life. There is the knowledge that one is in the presence of the Divine at every single moment of one's life.

Practice:

Contemplate that you are in the presence of the Divine at every single moment. Practice as often as you wish, but only for as long as the practice holds your interest. Observe how you choose to conduct your activities of life during this practice. Observe your level of contentment with life before, during, and after the practice.

Self-surrender: Self-surrender needs to be mastered in order to gain intuitive knowledge of any object of study, including the study of the Divine. One translation of this niyama is that self-surrender simply means worship of the Divine. There is a deeper meaning, however. At a stage of samādhi where one wishes to gain intuitive knowledge, consciousness must be merged with the object of study to understand the object as the object experiences itself. The sense of I-am-ness must be let go. This is a more subtle meaning of self-surrender.

Self-study: Self-study (svādhyāya) means to continually examine oneself and one's life with respect to whether life is being led according to the yamas and the niyamas. The purpose of this self-study is to ensure progress towards the goal of yoga. A more subtle meaning of svādhyāya is to keep consciousness focused on that Divine aspect of oneself.

XXXIII. When the mind is disturbed by improper or negative thoughts, one can practice pondering over the opposite.

Ohashi once told the story about his early days in America. He had worked his way from Japan to America on a cargo ship. After arriving in America he was quite depressed. He looked at several factors in his life. He was short. He was Japanese. He had no money. He contemplated those perceived shortcomings and came to some interesting conclusions. His insights helped with a sense of contentment, and also helped motivate him to pursue his path in life. He concluded that because he was short, he would not be a threat to anyone. He concluded that because he was Japanese, when he taught shiatsu everyone would consider the teaching to be genuine. He concluded that because he had no money, any money he would receive would feel like a great blessing. This contentment with his circumstance of life and some hard work allowed him to become a world renowned shiatsu instructor with centers of instruction all over the world. Surrender to one's circumstance in life can free the mind to pursue great things. Discontent can rob the mind of its energy and motivation.

Someone once asked the Dalai Lama how he felt about the Chinese and their invasion of Tibet. His reply, in part, was "I pray for their illumination." While one without such insight might feel anger or hatred toward those that had invaded one's homeland, mobilizing compassion and love in the mind is a sign of a more balanced perspective.

While a medical student in training, one of the first patients I saw was an East Indian gentleman who had been diagnosed with diabetes. I asked him how he felt about his diagnosis. To my surprise, he indicated his diagnosis of diabetes was a great blessing in that whenever he did something that he perhaps should not do, his blood sugar informed him right away of his error.

Practice:

Find an improper or negative thought, preferably a recurring thought. Then contemplate the opposite.

Something to consider:

Negative or improper thoughts, just like painful events, also have some capacity to teach us what we need to know in life.

XXXIV. Improper thoughts and actions, to whatever degree engaged in, result in the fruit of pain and misery. Such thoughts and actions are based on ignorance and are

often the result of greed, anger, or infatuation. Contemplating this and learning from this contemplation can free the mind.

Much of the misery and poverty on this earth are caused by jealousy (a form of anger combined with acquisitiveness) and greed. Someone wants what someone else has, whether it be territory, a spouse, or someone's wealth and possessions. Harmful thoughts or actions directed at another bear the fruits of pain and misery on this earth.

XXXV. If one is firmly established in nonviolence, there is abandonment of hostility in one's presence.

Mahatma Gandhi led a nation to freedom with this principle. This and the following sūtras describe the results of establishing the yamas and niyamas in one's life.

XXXVI. If one is firmly established in truth, the fruits of actions rest only on the yogi.

With the establishment of truthfulness and honesty, fearlessness follows. It is said in the Scriptures that if one is established in truth, all that is spoken will come true. It is also said that the things of the world will run after an honest person. He/she will not have to chase the things of the world.

Something to consider:

If one is not truthful with oneself, how can one expect to see and trust the truths experienced and learned on the path of yoga.

XXXVII. If one is firmly established in non-stealing, precious things present themselves.

Perhaps the most precious thing that presents itself is contentment and peace of mind. That contentment and peace of mind allows one to progress and may well serve one past the time that we spend in this current life.

XXXVIII. On being firmly established in Brahmacarya, energy and vigor is attained.

When one is not wasting oneself chasing the baubles of the world, the prāṇas and energy of life are free to help oneself in potentially miraculous ways.

XXXIX. Through being steady and non-possessive, one can know the hows and wherefores of birth and death (existence).

The attitude of non-possessiveness, even for life itself, allows one to be free of the fear of loss, including the fear of death with loss of the body. One can also lose the fear of surrendering one's sense of self, ego, I-am-ness. Such surrender is necessary in some stages of samādhi.

XL. By physical purification, one can feel disgust or desire for noncontact with the less physically pure.

Mastery is not there until one can maintain purity in the midst of filth including the presence of imperfections in one's own self. Recognizing the body, prāṇas, or mind as impure motivates one for change and leads one to try to avoid that in life which might amplify impurities. The food one chooses to eat, the people with whom one chooses to associate, or the circumstances in which one chooses to place oneself can all be influenced by the desire for noncontact with that which is less physically pure.

The desire for noncontact is without judgment. The cobra travels through the filth of the sewer, and yet remains clean. That which is touched in the sewer is simply not allowed to adhere.

XLI. From mental purity arises cheerful-mindedness, one-pointedness, control of the senses, and fitness for mystical vision of the Divine that is part of oneself.

The purity referred to in this sūtra reflects itself in thought, word, and deed. This leads to the quality of clarity, or sattva.

XLII. From contentment results an unexcelled joy.

XLIII. Austerities can result in perfection of body and sense organs after the destruction of impurities. This can result in siddhis (seemingly miraculous accomplishments).

The third section of the Yoga Sūtras, Vibhūti Pada, describes some of these accomplishments.

XLIV. By self-study, one achieves union with the desired deity.

There are two important points to consider in the study of this sūtra. Self-study does not mean just the study of Scriptures. It involves actually doing practices. When my teacher gave me a practice, he never told me I had to do it. But he was very clear that absence of any practice resulted in absence of any knowledge gained. If one wishes to understand all layers of oneself, one must do some practice.

The second point of this sūtra is that the Divine is not confined to any one particular form when making itself known to the consciousness of the seeker. While humanity sometimes goes to war with the excuse that one culture's concept of the Divine is superior to another culture's, the Divine has no culturally bound limitations of expression and revelation to the seeker.

XLV. The result of self-surrender to the Divine is samādhi.

This sūtra refers to gaining intuitive knowledge of the Divine by surrendering the sense of I-am-ness, our ordinary sense of identity, while establishing the focus of the mind on the Divine. One discipline adopted by practitioners is to contemplate doing everything in the name of the Divine. When one does everything with feeling of love for the Divine, one can mobilize a profound bliss leading to the state of samādhi.

My teacher described love as the most ancient traveler in the universe. All ages and cultures understand the language of love. When you speak googles and coos to an infant, the infant immediately understands that language of love. The sounds tend to be the same in all languages, and the love behind the sounds is understood in all cultures and all languages. It is the feeling of love that carries more meaning than the actual sounds of baby talk.

XLVI. Postures (āsanas) should be steady and comfortable.

Perhaps the most important phrase in the entire Yoga Sutras for hatha yogis, this sūtra defines the features indicating mastery of a particular pose. Comfortable and steady means not extending a pose to the point of experiencing a negative reaction. When an āsana is pushed to the point of creating pain, the body reacts. The first reaction of the body to pain is to tighten up muscles in order to splint the area. If pain is repeatedly created in a particular area, fascia thickens and becomes more scar-like. If thickening and becoming more stiff does not work, the body lays down calcium at the tendon attachments to bone in order to provide more support for the affected area. Radiologists call these bone spurs or degenerative changes.

The mind can also react to pain. If one creates pain for oneself every day, the mind eventually pushes forward and consciously or unconsciously says "Stop!" The practitioner may quit their hatha yoga practice without ever realizing why.

A potential obstacle for achieving comfort in a pose is chronic pain that is part of some medical conditions. One way to attend to the issue of chronic pain is to not raise pain levels more than two points on a ten point scale while doing a practice.

Hatha yoga creates changes to barriers of restriction through what osteopaths refer to as muscle energy techniques and myofascial release principles. Both of these direct and indirect agents of change work most effectively when barriers of restriction are first engaged, not when the practitioner has forcefully pushed through the barrier of restriction.

Overextending a pose can produce enough discomfort to distract the practitioner from attending to the more subtle prāṇic aspects of the pose. Stretching and compressing tissues during āsana practice creates subtle bioelectric field changes because of the nature of fascia being a liquid crystalline matrix. These changes can affect blockages and flows of prāṇa. The balance between the "ha" and the "tha", the right and the left prāṇas is also affected by āsana practice.

Practices:

1. Assume a pose and find where that pose can be maintained as both comfortable and steady.

2. Pick a pose and sense where you first feel a barrier of restriction beginning to engage. Hold the pose with even breathing and follow the barrier if it changes.

XLVII. By relaxation of effort (or natural tendency toward restlessness) and meditation on the "endless", or infinite, the posture is mastered.

To experience the meaning of the sūtra one can try a simple standing pose. Place the feet and knees together while rotating the pelvis posteriorly to pull the sacrum under the spine. Feel the spine becoming more erect as the chest lifts and the head and chin pull into a less forward position. When four landmarks are in the same plane (meatus or openings of the ears, acromion process of the shoulders, greater trochanters of the thighs, and malleoli of the ankles), hold the pose until there is no wobble in the soles of the feet.

Steadiness of posture is not possible without steadiness of mind. One of the ways to help establish steadiness of mind is to learn to pay attention to the prāṇas during any pose. The focus that the mind must achieve to attend to the subtle sensations of the prāṇas helps the mind to achieve that steadiness which will help the practitioner master the āsana. More is presented regarding sensing the prāṇas in sūtra XLIX.

XLVIII. From that (mastery) there can be no assault from the pairs of opposites.

Examples of the pairs of opposites referred to in this sūtra are the effects of heat and cold, joy and sorrow, illness and health, vigor and fatigue. One can remain neutral and balanced regardless of physical, energetic, or mental forces directed at the practitioner.

In 1996 my wife and I trekked to Gomuhk where the major tributary of the Ganges came roaring out of the ice cave in the glacier. Gomuhk is located upstream from Gangotri. The landscape at 13,500 feet elevation consists of rocks and boulders with no vegetation visible. The surrounding snow covered peaks rise another 10,000 feet above the river bed. In 1996 the glacier was about four km. north of Bhojwasa. We rested reclining on the top of a very large boulder well above the riverbed. The sun and rest were quite refreshing after the somewhat exhausting trek at high altitude. When we opened our eyes we noticed two things. The tour group with which we had trekked to the glacier had already left to return to the campsite at Bhojwasa. We also observed a number of very large birds circling above us, presumably wondering if we were dead and ready to be consumed.

As we started our descent back to the campground, it only took a few minutes for us to become lost from the path which had been barely discernible amongst the large boulders and rocks. We decided to follow the riverbed instead of trying to find the path. As we were passing an area where a swami was washing his saffron robes, he began to scold us for some reason. We heard a clap from farther up the hill where another older swami had clapped to get our attention. He motioned us to come up the hill where he had his abode. Where he lived was very simply constructed. A stick supported a sheet of corrugated metal. Flooring was made up of tarps and a blanket. There was a small cooking area where a pot could be suspended over a small fire. It did not escape our attention that we were in our layered expedition clothing while he sat comfortably in only a loincloth. While he did not speak to us as he was maintaining silence, he did write a few notes in response to our inquiries. He sketched some pictures of the visions he had had while meditating in that area the past sixteen years.

While we were seated with him, the large birds that had been circling us came and landed within 2 to 3 feet of us. They were very large black ravens, their bodies being as large as our torsos. They seemed content to sit perfectly still as we conversed. The swami used his meager cooking utensils to prepare some potato parathas (pan-fried Indian flatbread) for us. He indicated his diet consisted of one potato a day and some powdered milk in boiled water.

We had asked the swami about his meditation practices. He indicated that he would sit on a rock in the Ganges from midnight until 6:00 AM each morning. We asked if he got cold. He indicated he would sometimes use a blanket to cover himself during that time. The night before when we had stayed in Bhojwasa, the temperature had been 25 degrees Fahrenheit and it had been snowing. Sūtra XLVIII describes a practitioner's ability to master responses to stimuli. This may lead to such abilities as to be immune to external stimuli, such as heat or cold, as this adept had apparently mastered.

XLIX. Once a comfortable and steady posture has been acquired, the movements of inhalation and exhalation should be controlled. This is prāṇāyāma.

The usual translation given for prāṇāyāma is regulation or restraint of the prāṇas. While the breath is not prāṇa, it is a vehicle for that energy called prāṇa. One can work with the vehicle of the breath to manage the prāṇas, or one can work with direct perception of the flows, rhythms, and restrictions of prāṇa to facilitate one's progress on the path of yoga.

After one has practiced diaphragmatic breathing for a time (commentary on Samādhi Pada, sūtra XIII), one can add the following practices:

Alternate nostril breathing (nādī ṣodhana) is a practice for cleansing or purifying (ṣodhana) the energy channels (nādīs). The phrase, nādī ṣodhana, is also sometimes translated as purification of the nervous system. One goal of this practice is to get the left (iḍā) and right (piṅgalā) energy channels to flow more evenly.

Practice:

In the practice of alternate nostril breathing we set up gentle rhythms of exhaling warmth and inhaling coolness. This has a calming effect on the mind and prepares us for practices of equalizing the flow of breath in the nostrils. The flow of the breath should be smooth (steady). The length of the breath should be comfortable with inhalation and exhalation of equal length. The practice is performed in a seated position

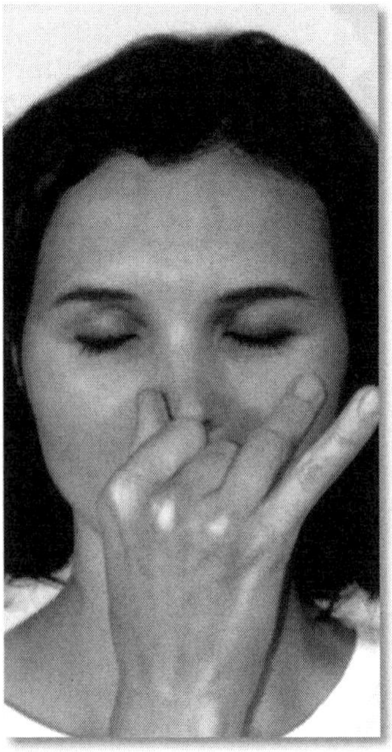

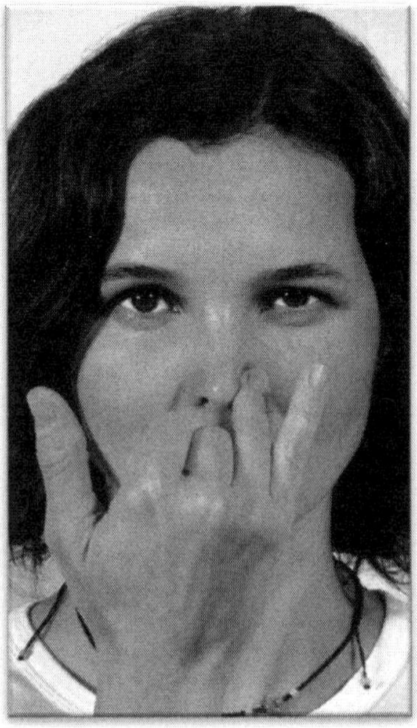

unless the person cannot sit for medical reasons.

With the head, neck, and trunk erect, the right arm is bent at the elbow and the right shoulder is relaxed. The right thumb is used to close off the right nostril as we exhale and then inhale through the left nostril. The right fourth and/or fifth fingers are used to close off the left nostril as we exhale and inhale through the right nostril.

There are many variations of this technique. The common thread of these techniques is to exhale and inhale the same number of times with each nostril in a symmetric pattern. A simple pattern is to exhale and inhale one breath through one nostril, then switch and exhale and inhale through the opposite nostril. Keep switching nostrils after each inhalation. Many other patterns of alternate nostril breathing are taught in various yoga traditions.

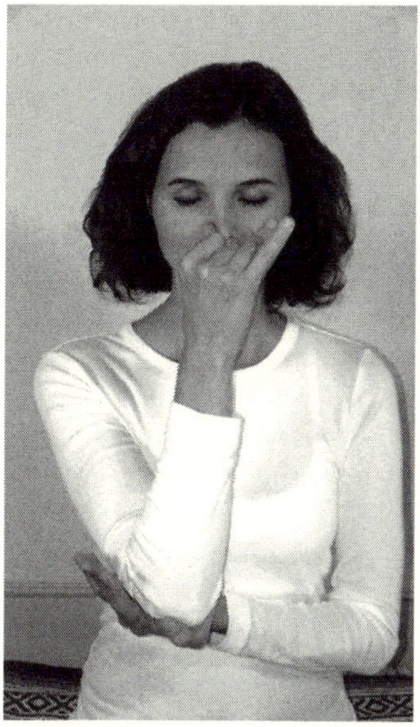

If the arm and shoulder tire easily, use the left hand to support the right elbow. Women generally find that placing the left forearm under the breasts and elevating the forearm into position is more comfortable than placing the forearm over the breasts. The outer edge of the heel of the hand will fit nicely against the right lower ribs while cradling the right elbow or right upper arm.

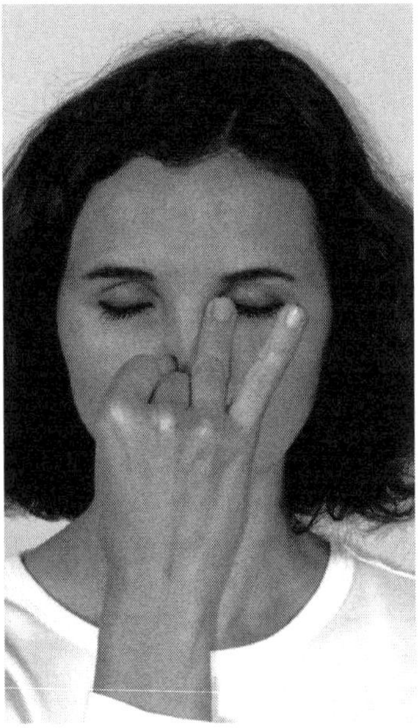

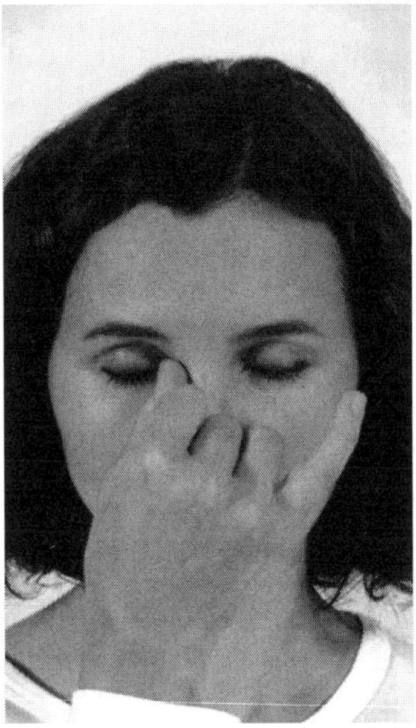

Practice in front of a mirror or video camera at first as there is a tendency to pull the head to the right when practicing this technique. One way to minimize this tendency is to use the thumb over the right side of the bony ridge of the nose when closing the left nostril with the fourth and fifth finger, and use the fourth finger over the left side of the bony ridge of the nose while closing the right nostril with the thumb (see above pictures).

There are many descriptions about which nostril to start with at which time of the day. One common prescription is to start the practice by exhaling through the dominant nostril.

The technique is best practiced in the morning before having eaten and in the evening before bed. It can also be done an additional time during the day. Generally it is done a minimum of three breaths with each nostril. When done before meditation it has a significant quieting effect on the mind. The reason for this calming effect may have to do with rhythmic variation in rates of neural firing from the neurons of the olfactory bulbs in the nasal cavity to the preseptal area of the brain. This has a potential effect on changing the rhythmicity of firing in the limbic system. The limbic system has some regulating effect on the reticular activating system. The reticular activating system influences level of focus, whether someone is awake or asleep, whether someone is alert, in a stupor, or comatose. The reticular activating system also influences regulation of parasympathetic and sympathetic nervous systems, helping one manage one's state of relaxation.

The body naturally alternates the rhythm of breath without conscious assistance. At any given time one nostril is more dominant than the other in terms of openness and airflow allowed. This dominance shifts every one to three hours on average throughout the twenty-four hour day. Meditators who have studied these breath rhythms extensively also note dominance changes depending on such things as phases of the moon and activities engaged in. They also describe that in states of meditation the nostrils can flow absolutely equally with a profound effect on the ability to focus on subtle phenomena.

How often does one practice the alternate nostril breathing? For several months in the mid 1970's I did the experiment of practicing nādī ṣodhana twice daily, three times daily, or four times daily all for several months for each frequency of practice. I noticed a significant increase in my focusing abilities when practicing three times daily versus practicing only twice daily. I would notice that my ability to establish the smoothness of serene breath and my ability to focus on more subtle aspects of yoga practice improved. I did not notice any additional benefit increasing the practice to four times daily. This is not a scientific study, only a difference noted in my own practice.

How long does one practice the technique? In my practice I perform at least three breaths in each nostril. If I do less than that, I notice no effect. Practice as long as the technique appears to be beneficial and holds your interest. If one bores oneself with one's practice, the mind builds up unconscious resistance which can result in dropping one's practice altogether.

To help smooth the breath, one can add the mantra "SoHam," exhaling to the sound of "ham" and inhaling to the sound of "so." The practice of nādī ṣodhana can help to balance the physiological response to surprise in one's meditation practice as one discovers new aspects of oneself on a more subtle level.

Practice:

The more subtle aspects of prāṇāyāma practice involve differentiating the flow of the breath from the activities of the prāṇas. To become aware of the prāṇas, one can improve the ability of the mind to focus on increasingly subtle aspects of the breath. The following practices relate to more directly experiencing the prāṇas. This helps in learning how to separate the sensations of breath from the sensations of the prāṇas.

Once one has improved the smoothness of flow of the breath, one can begin to focus on the sensations of airflow in the nostrils. Look first for the sensations of airflow and then for the sensations of coolness as one inhales and warmth as one exhales. This practice is done with an erect spine in either a seated pose or lying supine in śavāsana. To refine the practice further, contain the mind within the hollow space of the dominant nostril. During inhalation find the exact point in that hollow space that feels the absolute coolest. Narrow the focus to the size of the head of a pin. Then pay attention to the temperature changes at that single point, coolness at that point on the inhale and warmth at that point on the exhale. After a few breaths, perform the same exercise focusing on the hollow of the opposite nostril. This practice will allow one to distinguish two separate air flows, one in each nostril.

Practice:

This practice is a follow-up to the practice given in verse one of Samādhi Pada. To begin to distinguish the flows of prāṇas, focus on the silent space between the two air flows of the nostrils, that space where there is no airflow. In this quiet space, one can attend to the flow of prāṇa. Prāṇa moves upward and inward during inhalation and apāṇa moves downward and outward through this space during exhalation. Another more subtle rhythm of prāṇa can also be felt in this quiet space. The continuous dance between "ha" and "tha", the right and left energies of piṅgalā and iḍā can also be felt in the space between the air flows of the nostrils. Feeling this energy dance in the area of the nose bridge between the two air flows is one place to look for the dance between piṅgalā and iḍā. One can also look for the dance at the indentation above the upper lip. Observe between the left and right prominences of the upper lip that define the indentation between the upper lip and the nose. The third place my teacher told us to look for the dance between piṅgalā and iḍā was between the energy orbs defined by the two eyes. These energy orbs are the subtle two petals of ājñā cakra.

The following is a diagram representing some of the major aspects of our prāṇas.

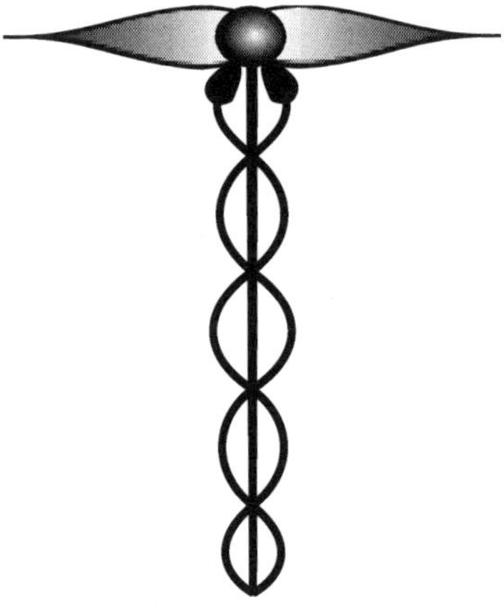

Pictured at the top of the diagram is ājñā cakra with its two lotus petals. Spiraling around the central energy channel, suṣumnā, are the left and right nādīs of iḍā and piṅgalā. Some will recognize this diagram as the caduceus, a symbol of healthcare around the world. Most health practitioners, however, have forgotten that it is a diagram representing the human energy system of nādīs and cakras. The left and right spiraling energies are often depicted as snakes. This is because the nādīs of iḍā and piṅgalā are constantly dancing with each other. If focus is applied in a way where this dance comes to stillness, or union, the gateway to suṣumnā becomes available and the central energy of the diagram, usually depicted as a dormant staff or rod, becomes active and allows the practitioner to experience a meditative state called suṣumnā awareness.

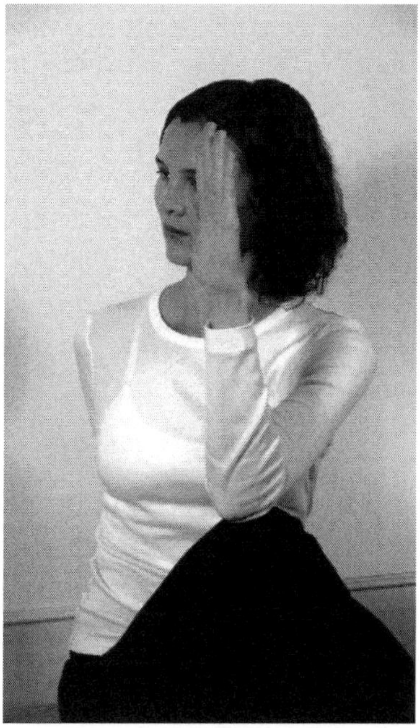

Practice:

If one has difficulty feeling the prāṇas, one can practice feeling the differences in nostril dominance during certain poses. At any given time, the flow of air in one nostril will be greater than the flow of the air in the opposite nostril. This dominance shifts every one to three hours for most people. In the spinal twist, however, if one has the major cakras properly lined up and turns one's head to the right, the left nostril will become more dominant in its flow. Postures affect the prāṇas. Prāṇas, in turn, affect the flow of breath in the nostrils. While breath is generally considered the vehicle for prāṇa, the energy of the prāṇas also reflects in the pattern of the breath. Becoming aware of the subtle changes in breath patterns can help one developed the sensitivity necessary to directly perceive the prāṇas.

L. Modifications of breath and prāṇāyāma practice are either external, internal, or stationary. The breath is to be regulated by space, time, and number and are either long or short in duration. Through practice the breath may become both prolonged and subtle.

This sūtra refers to various practices which might involve retention. When one has mastered inhalation and exhalation, under the guidance of the teacher retention might be added after inhalation, after exhalation, or after both. The sūtra also states that with practice the breath can be lengthened and the more subtle aspects of breath and prāṇa can be perceived. Below are some examples of progression in training in some of the practices of prāṇāyāma. It is not a comprehensive guide. It is offered as a general guideline to experienced yoga practitioners and is not meant for those just beginning the practice of hatha yoga. While the following is the way I was taught to do these practices, one should consult with one's own teacher before undertaking the steps below, particularly those steps involving retention practices. Retention practices carry medical risk and it is important to proceed with these practices under the guidance of an experienced teacher.

Step 1: Purifying the Nāḍis

One cannot master the breath without purifying the nāḍis with the practice of nāḍi ṣodhana. It is advisable to lengthen the time of practice of nāḍi ṣodhana for several months prior to undertaking retention practice. Recommended amount is at least 18 breaths two to three times per day.

Step 2: Lengthening the Breath

Try to lengthen both inhalation and exhalation while keeping them equal in the posture of śavāsana or in a seated meditation posture. Make certain the position assumed is both comfortable and steady, and that the ribcage does not compress the abdomen. For many the timing of breath in deep relaxation will be 2-3 breaths per minute or less. If you wish to know your capacity for length of breath, watch the second hand of a clock and see what timing of breath is comfortable when you slow the breath down for 3-5 minutes. I do not advise trying to count in the mind, as this produces a pause or fluctuation in breath with each count. Some count their heartbeats, but heart rate changes with the phase of the breath and can also become a distraction.

Step 3: Lengthening Exhalation

Practice lengthening exhalation until it is approximately twice as long as inhalation. Do not be impatient with this. From time to time, again use a clock to check the progress of what breath rate is comfortable for you to maintain for a few minutes. Your capacity may actually be for a longer breath with your eyes closed and attending internally, rather than externally, but it is difficult to see the clock then. Practice lengthening the breath and lengthening exhalation until one is comfortable with a 2:1 ratio of exhalation to inhalation with inhalation lasting 15-16 seconds and exhalation 30-32 seconds before attempting retention.

Step 4: Ābhyantara Kumbhaka – Internal Retention

Practice a brief retention after inhalation while practicing 2:1 breathing of Step 3 above. Gradually increase the length of the retention but always make certain the ratio is comfortable to maintain for three to five minutes. This does not mean you need to practice for that length of time each day, but the ratio should always be at a comfortable level with exhalation twice as long as inhalation. A beginning ration of 8 sec. inhalation: 4 sec. retention: 16 sec. exhalation might be an appropriate beginning ratio. Once a ratio of 16 inhalation: 32 retention: 32 exhalation is attained, maintain this ratio for some months before attempting to increase retention incrementally until a ratio of 16 inhalation: 64 retention: 32 exhalation is maintained comfortably.

Continue the practices that keep the breath mechanism fluid and maximally functional. It is also helpful to practice such techniques as ujjayi, kapālabhāti, and bhastrika prior to retention practice, both to increase blood flow and oxygenation prior to retention, but also for the more long-term benefit of conditioning the lungs for maximum exchange of oxygen and carbon dioxide at all levels of the lungs. Some teachers also recommend interspersing breathing without retention between periods of breathing with retention practices to keep from overextending.

With ujjayi, kapālabhāti, and bhastrika, as with any muscular activity, one can see training effects in muscles or development of problems from overextending oneself. Trigger points in abdominal musculature can occur, particularly if one does not do some self-bodywork on the muscle layers of the abdomen and myofascial release of the diaphragm and accessory muscles of breathing. Weakening of the connective tissue that joins the rectus muscles centrally can also occur with too vigorous practice or from pre-existing weakness of that structure, resulting in umbilical herniation.

A muscle often overlooked in the practice of retention is the diaphragm. One can lock this muscle after internal retention and unlock before exhalation, just as one locks it for the stomach lift. The feeling is the same, even though done after inhalation instead of after exhalation. If one strains while practicing this technique, however, there is some risk of producing atrial flutter or fibrillation as the lower chambers of the heart stop beating. Locking the diaphragm after exhalation is a safer technique to practice as in the stomach lift, nauli, or agni sara, until one is comfortable locking the diaphragm without contraction of associated musculature. When one has mastered this after exhalation and the practices of various versions of nauli and agni sara, then one might consider practicing the lock after internal retention under the guidance of a teacher.

Special Considerations and Practices:

Pay particular attention to the end of inhalation when doing serious practice of prāṇāyāma. It is the part of the breath that is most neglected when one is doing retention practice. A notable increase in breath capacity is possible when one frees up the final part of inhalation and one does not unconsciously create tension that restricts that final phase of inhalation. Most people have a habit of stopping short of full inhalation. One can also notice a sense of peace and calming if one does not restrict the final phase of inhalation where the diaphragm is maximally contracted. It may also be easier to lock the diaphragm when maximal contraction of the diaphragm is achieved.

Prāṇāyāma tends to have significant energizing effects and it is advisable to limit stimulants during periods where one is intensifying that phase of yoga practice. Metabolism also tends to increase when one increases breath practices involving the vigorous abdominal techniques, and more nourishing foods may be required during that time.

If one is focusing on prāṇāyāma practices, it is best to learn to feel the changes in prāṇa, and not just limit awareness to the ratios and physical aspects of the breath. Learning to experience prāṇa directly can greatly enhance the experience and understanding of prāṇāyāma.

LI. That prāṇāyāma which goes beyond the sphere of internal and external is the fourth variety.

The sūtra refers to the practice of kevala kumbhaka. During kevala kumbhaka the practitioner enters a conscious state where there is no longer a need to breathe in the normal manner. It is very similar to a near-death experience where an energy source is capable of supporting the practitioner's consciousness and physiology for an extended period of time without the body needing to exchange normal amounts of air as in everyday breathing. To enter the state one must not only bring the dance between iḍā and piṅgalā to stillness, but one also must bring prāṇa and apāṇa to balance.

LII. From those practices of prāṇāyāma the covering of light is dissolved.

Some commentators interpret this sūtra to mean that if one performs the aforementioned practices of the previous sūtras, one removes the veil of ignorance over the inner light.

There is another interpretation of this sūtra, however, that has practical guidance for those who have experiences in meditation involving fields of color or light. It is not uncommon as one progresses along the path of meditation to have fields of color or light come into view. If one is attending to the subtle prāṇas, one may notice these experiences occur more often as the left and right energies come more into balance.

If the activation of suṣumnā awareness is established when the field of color or light appears, that field of color or light may resolve in different ways. One way that it can resolve is to take the form of lotus petals which then open centrally to reveal something. There is also another way that the field of color or light can resolve. If one establishes and maintains the energetic balance associated with suṣumnā awareness, one can witness what appears initially to be a solid field of color to actually be a fine pattern of light. If suṣumnā awareness is maintained, the dark spaces in the pattern of light become clear and consciousness passes through one of those dark spaces to view what that veil of light was covering.

Similarly, when one begins to witness nādīs in deeper states of meditation, the nādīs can initially appear as ribbons of light when viewed externally. If one consciously enters a nādī, however, one might witness the nādī as being dark centrally and bordered by a pattern of light.

LIII. Another result of the aforementioned practices is that the mind becomes fit for dhāraṇā (concentration). The density of the mind (prāṇas and affect attached to saṃskāras) is reduced to allow more perfect concentration.

The result of prāṇāyāma practice is that the mind is less likely to jump around and change its focus while trying to practice meditation.

LIV. Pratyāhāra - detaching the mind from responding to external stimuli through the sense organs.

Practice:

One method to achieve pratyāhāra is AUM kriya. After one has learned to sense the flows of prāṇa and apāṇa, one can practice the following method effectively. The practice is done in śavāsana. Remember that "śava" means corpse. A result of practicing AUM kriya is to consciously experience the characteristics of a corpse, namely stillness and absence of sensory perception.

While lying in śavāsana, establish diaphragmatic breathing. Become aware of the flows of prāṇas ascending and descending in the more external central channel connecting the cakras. The more internal aspect of the central channel is suṣumnā nādī. Around this internal aspect are the flows of prāṇa and apāṇa, prāṇa flowing upward with inhalation, and apāṇa flowing downward with exhalation. Initially one can simply follow the flows upward and downward as far as consciousness wishes to go through the chain of cakras. This may simply be feeling the flow through one or two of the cakras, or may involve all the cakras. Consciousness may also wish to flow downward on the exhale through the root cakra (mūlādhāra cakra). Rather than trying to follow the flow of prāṇa down the extremities, keep awareness on the central channel that extends downward between the knees, ankles, and feet. There is a nodal point of energy along that central channel between the knees, and also between the ankles and feet.

The mantra "Om" has three syllables "A", "U", and "M". When practicing AUM kriya it is important to make the transitions between the three syllables as smooth as possible. The practice involves the use of this mantra while focusing on the flows of prāṇa and apāṇa. Begin the practice after establishing diaphragmatic breathing and balancing the flow of breath in the left and right nostrils, bringing iḍā and piṅgalā as close to balance as possible. Follow the flow of breath from ājñā cakra to the crown cakra (sahasrāra). Then begin exhaling and following apāṇa from sahasrāra through the chain of cakra's all the way down to a point between the ankles and feet. Let the mind focus internally on the sound "A" at sahasrāra, transitioning to "U" at the throat (viśuddha) cakra, and then transitioning to the sound "M" as one follows the flow of apāṇa downward. Exhalation should be at least twice as long as inhalation.

On the inhalation one follows the flow of prāṇa upward beginning with the sound "A" at the feet, transitioning to "U" at the throat, and then transitioning to the sound "M" to sahasrāra cakra. On both the upward and downward flow one transitions to the sound "U" at the throat cakra. Initially the breath may not feel long enough to exhale and reach between the feet. One can practice between the crown cakra and mūlādhāra cakra for a time with the breath ratio of 2:1 exhalation to inhalation before lengthening and extending the exhalation to reach between the feet. Sensing the prāṇas in this manner can lead to feelings of joy and lightness. After practicing this method for some time, one may get the sense that one is pulling energy in from the cosmos as one inhales. Extending the exhalation past the feet may help accentuate that experience. If suṣumnā awareness is established during this practice, one can very quickly go to that silence where there is no longer input from the body's usual senses. This is a state of pratyāhāra. When one is ready to come out of the practice, exhalation is shortened again to a more normal breath ratio of 2:1 or less until one is feeling the flows only between ājñā cakra and sahasrāra cakra. The breath may be very fine and nearly imperceptible at that point.

A few cautions are necessary for this practice. When one comes out of the practice, it is important to do so gradually. When the body is in such a state of immobility and deep relaxation, tendons and ligaments can become strained if one suddenly moves when first coming out of the practice. For this reason it is also important to pick a place and circumstance where one is not likely to be suddenly interrupted.

LV. Then follows the greatest mastery over the senses.

All of your senses come under complete voluntary control. The bodily senses will no longer have the capacity to disturb the seeker.

Vibhūti Pāda

Vibhūti is generally translated as the accomplishments or by-products of yoga practice. The following are an exposition of the accomplishments or results of yoga practices.

I. Dhāraṇā - confining the mind to a limited mental area (place, object, or idea).

Dhāraṇā is generally translated as concentration. It is not, however, concentration in the usual sense of one attempting to focus. Dhāraṇā refers to perfected concentration where the mind's attention is fixed on only one idea, object of focus, or content. There are still breaks in awareness as the universe refreshes itself in its continual pattern of resolving itself into the void and then re-emerging with seeming sameness. The refresh rate for the universe is much higher than can be observed during ordinary states of consciousness and in the state of dhāraṇā. It is much like the refresh rate on a computer screen or television where the image on the screen appears to be an unbroken continuous flow despite the known refresh rate on the screen where the picture disappears and reappears sixty or more times per second.

II. Dhyāna - uninterrupted flow of the mind toward an object.

During dhyāna not only is perfect concentration accomplished as in dhāraṇā, but there is also the elimination of the momentary breaks in awareness that imperceptibly occur in time with the refresh rate described in the previous sūtra. The total content of the mind upon which one is focused at a given moment is held in conscious awareness continuously over time. This eliminates the momentary breaks as pratyaya, the total content of the mind, remains fixed as the sole object of focus. Dhyāna is generally translated as meditation. Dhyāna, the goal of many varied meditation techniques, quickly leads to samādhi. While meditation is often defined in our culture as many different techniques, dhyāna is the goal sought by these different techniques. One technique of meditation is the following practice.

Practice:

1. Establish diaphragmatic breathing (Samādhi Pada XIII).

2. Attend to the flow of the breath in the nostrils, feeling the coolness on the inhale and the warmth on the exhale.

3. Balance the left and the right prāṇas, allowing the right and left nostrils to flow equally.

4. Find a stream of coolness in each nostril. Find a distinct stream of cool air flow on inhalation in each nostril.

5. As you inhale, follow the two streams of coolness to an area of joining deep in the nasal cavity. Spend a few breaths sensing the transitions between warmth on the exhale and coolness on the inhale at that area of joining.

6. During inhalation follow that coolness inward and downward to the area of the larynx. At any time during the practice, one can merge the mantra "soham" with the breath. Spend a few breaths in the area of the larynx sensing the temperature changes on inhalation and exhalation. Look for the exact moments of temperature change to deepen the focus.

7. Now, inhale and follow the coolness down to the deepest point. If the diaphragmatic contraction is complete, your tactile awareness will be led near an energy point called hṛt (pronounced hrit) within the radiance of anāhata cakra. Spend a few breaths focusing on this point.

8. Once hṛt has been located, find another energy point called dvādaṣāṅta located four finger widths anterior to the area of the thorax where the lowest ribs join the sternum. Exhale from the energy point hṛt into the radiance of anāhata cakra to dvādaṣāṅta. Inhale back to hṛt. This step eight is one of the practices from the text "Vijñāna Bhairāva". Not given in that text is the use of the mantra "soham" as described in step nine.

9. This step requires focusing directly on the prāṇa flow. Prāṇa dhāraṇā is translated as focus or concentration on the prāṇas or of concentration of the prāṇas. The practice of prāṇa dhāraṇā involves direct perception of the prāṇas rather than focusing on breath as one vehicle or carrier of prāṇa. A subtle flow of prāṇa connects the two energy points of hṛt and dvādaṣāṅta. This flow of prāṇa moves anteriorly from hṛt to dvādaṣāṅta in time with exhalation. The prāṇa flow moves posteriorly from dvādaṣāṅta to hṛt in time with inhalation. Merge the vibration of the mantra "soham" with the subtle flow of prāṇa. (An introduction to sensing the energy of the prāṇas is presented in the commentary on sūtra XXVI.)

III. Consciousness only of the object of meditation, not of oneself (mind) is samādhi.

In samādhi, the knowledge of what is studied is no longer colored by the interpretation of one's mind. The mind is full of influences, both conscious as well as unconscious, which can affect the interpretation of what is observed. When the energy of those influences has been reduced to null (citta-vṛitti-nirodha), there remains only consciousness of the object of meditation. The state of samādhi is a prerequisite for gaining intuitive knowledge of the object of study, namely merging consciousness with that object and experiencing the object of meditation as the object experiences itself.

IV. Dhāraṇā, dhyāna, and samādhi taken together constitute saṃyama.

The by-product of saṃyama, the simultaneous practice of dhāraṇā, dhyāna, and samādhi upon a content of mind can be the siddhis, the paranormal powers which come to yogis naturally through their advanced practice.

V. By mastering saṃyama comes the light of higher consciousness.

The truth behind the object of study becomes known. It is this knowledge of the truth that allows siddhis to become known to the practitioner.

VI. Saṃyama is accomplished in stages.

The practitioner masters saṃyama by practicing the stages leading up to it, namely dhāraṇā, dhyāna, and samādhi.

VII. The three limbs of yoga taken together (dhāraṇā, dhyāna, and samādhi) are internal in relation to the five preceding limbs of yoga (yamas, niyamas, āsana, prāṇāyāma, and pratyāhāra).

The yoga of eight limbs known as aṣtānga yoga has the three internal limbs of concentration (dhāraṇā), meditation (dhyāna), and samādhi as well as the preceding limbs of attitudes (yamas), observances (niyamas), postures (āsanas), practices for regulating the prāṇas (prāṇāyāma), and sense withdrawal (pratyāhāra).

VIII. Sabīja samādhi is external to nirbīja samādhi.

Practice of saṃyama and sabīja samādhi (with seed or content of mind) are more external then nirbīja samādhi (without seed).

IX. Nirodha pariṅāma is that transformation of the mind where the mind becomes progressively permeated by nirodha (that which intervenes momentarily between an impression in the mind that is disappearing and another impression that is appearing).

This sūtra describes the state of transformation that occurs as a result of suppression of the modifications of the mind (citta-vṛitti-nirodha). The mind has momentary breaks between one impression, or content, of the mind and a subsequent impression of the mind. Nirodha is that state between impressions where there is no content of mind.

X. The flow of nirodha state becomes tranquil (steady) with repeated practice.

A difficult practice is to maintain a state of mind where no impression emerges to occupy the mind's attention. The state of nirodha, the space between impressions, becomes the focus of the mind. Through this practice, the state of nirodha itself becomes the content of the mind, and in so doing, becomes elongated and preserves the state of nirodha.

The sages of many traditions advise us to bring the mind to a state of silence. When the mind practices one-pointedness, ekāgratā, on absolute silence, one can consciously experience the union of divine potential with the force of creation in order to create an impression for the mind of something not previously known by the practitioner, or perhaps not previously known by anyone. Sometimes students, however, are taught to actually resist the mind going to silence. For example, they are taught to hang on to their mantras at any cost, even when the mind naturally wants to go to silence. Paraphrasing what my teacher used to say, "When you are waiting for the bus (doing japa), and the bus finally comes, get on the bus. There may not be another bus for a long time, or perhaps ever."

Practice:

When the mind is drawn to that absolute silence with ekāgratā, let the mind dwell there.

XI. The development of consciousness toward samādhi is facilitated by settling of distraction and simultaneous arising of one-pointedness.

XII. Ekāgratā pariṅāma is a condition of the mind when what arises in the mind is exactly similar to that which subsided.

Ekāgratā pariṅāma is generally translated as one-pointedness on a temporary state of mind. The state of dhāraṇā (perfect concentration) is one example of ekāgratā pariṅāma. The state of dhyāna, the continuous focus without break (no disappearance and re-emergence of the mind's impression) on a single content of mind, quickly leads to the state of samādhi.

Paralleling the state of the mind called ekāgratā pariṅāma is the state of the world and the universe. The content of the universe subsides to the undefined, and re-emerges to seemingly the same content many times per second. The nature of the universe is vibratory in that sense. It is that vibratory nature that allows the universe to evolve and change over time. Similarly, the mind has a vibratory component of disappearance and re-emergence. It is during the re-emergence that the mind has the potential to change its content. The mind can be trained so that the content of the mind that reemerges is the same as the content that previously disappeared.

XIII. By the previous four sūtras, the properties (time factors), visible characteristics, and condition of transformations in the elements and sense organs are also explained.

This sūtra provides the reminder that the practices of transmutation and transformation that are part of many of the accomplishments, or siddhis, have as their basis an understanding of the principles described in the foregoing sūtras. When I traveled to Varanasi in 1995, I had a chance to visit what I was told was a center of left hand tantra in Varanasi. As our group approached the gate, I noted an absence of the usual images of deities seen at the entrance of most temples. The grounds of this temple, Krim Kund, were guarded only by the statues of skulls.

The pandit I was with mumbled a few mantras at the gate and we proceeded inside, removing our shoes near the gate. As we moved toward the central portion of the compound, I noted a thickness of energy. It was almost as if one were moving through a liquid rather than through air. The next thing I noticed was a dog playing with a deer near the talab (pool of water). Running quickly around the border of the talab was a mongoose. We visited and did some meditation by the fire pit that was described as having been continuously burning for several hundred years, serving as a place of ritual and worship for the aghoras (practitioners of left hand tantra) who had trained at this particular ashram.

We then sat on a shaded and raised platform in the compound where we had lunch and listened to the words of the current head of that particular ashram. He read from the diary of the recently departed master of the left hand tantra tradition at Krim Kund. In the diary was a beautiful definition of the path of left hand tantra, the path of aghora. The practice of left hand tantra is to take that which is of filth, bad, impure, or unbalanced and transmute and transform it into that which is beautiful, pure, good, and in balance through the application of the power of overwhelming love and compassion.

The accomplishments, powers, or siddhis are cautioned by many teachers to be distractions on the path of yoga. As I was taught, the siddhis are not a distraction when they are used in the service of others as part of one's duties while traveling the path of life. The siddhis can, however, become a distraction if used only for personal enjoyment or gain.

XIV. Dharmī - the substratum in which the latent, active, or unmanifest properties inhere.

An example of the three properties spoken about in this sūtra would be a seed. The seed has the latent potential to grow into a flower, vegetable, or tree. The active property would be the manifestation that we would sense as a flower, vegetable, or tree. The potential to become a seed would be the unmanifest state of the seed, flower, vegetable, or tree. The "substratum" of this sūtra would be prakṛiti, that aspect of the universe which is manifest. Dharmī is the property holder, the nature of that which is the thing in past (potential to become, e.g. seed), present (current form, e.g. plant or tree), and future forms (fruit or vegetable that might come from the plant or tree).

XV. The cause of the difference in transformation is the difference in the underlying process, the natural law differences.

The seed in the above sūtra has the capacity to be a plant bearing flowers, fruit, and leaves. The clay of the earth has the capacity to be transformed into a brick or a clay pot. The difference in the form taken is dependent upon the natural laws governing the process of transformation into the brick or the clay pot, or a flower bearing plant that then becomes a fruit bearing plant.

XVI. By performing saṃyama on the three kinds of transformation or stages of evolution (nirodha pariṅāma, samādhi pariṅāma, and ekāgratā pariṅāma.), one obtains knowledge of the past and future.

Knowing the process of transformation from an experiential perspective through the application of saṃyama (simultaneous application of concentration, meditation, and samādhi on an object of focus) allows the understanding of the process of time and time's effect on a particular object or content of mind.

Nirodha pariṅāma refers to the process of the evolution of the mind. Complete understanding of how the mind transforms from one content of mind to another content of mind allows understanding of the evolution of thought and feelings.

Samādhi pariṅāma refers to the process of evolution of consciousness. Consciously remaining aware and understanding the nature of the transitions of the mind between waking, dreaming, and deep sleep would be an example. Consciously understanding the evolution of consciousness through the various forms of samādhi would be another example.

Ekāgratā pariṅāma refers to the process of evolution of the universe and the perception of that universe. Consciously experiencing the vibratory nature of the universe with its reabsorption and re-emergence many times per second would be an example.

Understanding the above processes of transformation allows perception of the trends in transformation. This awareness allows understanding of the origins of current experience in the present, which would be the past leading up to the present moment. Understanding the process of transformation on the different levels mentioned in this sūtra also lets on know the likely trend of future experience.

XVII. By performing saṃyama on the sound, the meaning and the idea behind the utterance of any living being can be known.

The meaning of words in any language can be discerned. The utterance of any animal or living thing can be understood.

XVIII. Knowledge of previous birth can be obtained by direct perception of impressions through the performance of saṃyama on those impressions.

The siddhis are not all listed individually in the Yoga Sūtras. Remember that the mind contains impressions of everything in the universe on either a conscious or an unconscious level. Through the process of performing saṃyama, one can potentially know anything. For example, by performing saṃyama on the previously unconscious impressions of a past life, one can gain knowledge of their previous life.

XIX. One can obtain knowledge of the mind of others through direct perception of the image occupying the mind.

Remember that a thought in anyone's mind also leaves an impression in the practitioner's mind.

XX. By accomplishing the saṃyama described in the previous sūtra, one does not necessarily observe the mental

factors (motive, etc.) behind the image of the mind perceived.

XXI. Saṃyama on the body's form (rūpa) and suspension of the receptive power (sight), contact between the eye and the observer is broken and the body becomes invisible.

If the projection of the light or image from that which is to be observed by another is broken, the object can no longer be seen. One can become invisible to others.

XXII. By the same process, sound can be made to disappear.

XXIII. By performing saṃyama on portents and on the active and dormant karmas - knowledge of time of death.

Karmas are generally considered to be of three types. Saṃcita karma is the total stock of karmas. Hence, saṃcita karma includes all of one's individual karma as well as everyone's karma since in the view of yoga, we are all contained within each other. It is only the illusion of our individual identity that allows us to see each other as separate beings. Through the circumstance and process of birth, we are granted a portion of the total karma to be worked out in this lifetime. Life is a collection of opportunities and obstacles through which to work out this life's karma. Prārabdha karma is that karma to be dealt with in one's current life. Kriyamāṇa karma is that karma which is generated day by day. That karma may be dealt with in the current lifetime, or may be added to the storehouse of saṃcita karma.

Regarding performing saṃyama on portents, my teacher used to say that preceding events happening on a physical level, there would be an energetic shift that if attended to, would allow one to know what was about to happen. The clues to future events, or portents, can be read by performing saṃyama on those energetic shifts or clues.

XXIV. Performing saṃyama on friendliness results in the strengthening of that quality.

By strengthening a quality in oneself, that quality may also be transferred. The quality of charisma, for example, can be a result of strengthening the quality of friendliness within oneself and having that quality also transfer to others.

XXV. Saṃyama of strength (or qualities in general) results in the strengthening of that quality.

Performing saṃyama on the strength of an elephant, for example, might lead to superhuman strength. Performing saṃyama on a feather, a piece of lint floating in the air, or the quality of lightness in any object might grant the ability to fly.

XXVI. Knowledge of the small (the subtle), the hidden, or the distant by directing the light of superphysical faculty (performing saṃyama on the light within).

Some of the healing practices in yoga depend upon the ability to see within oneself or someone else, visualizing the internal gross anatomy and subtle anatomy (on a cellular or molecular level as well as on an energetic level). Effective distance healing depends on the ability to accurately image the gross and subtle anatomy of the subject. Many of the miracles of healing reported to be performed have this sūtra as a basis.

Practices:

1. If you wish to begin to build the perception of the subtle, try the following exercise. Remember the terms most often used to describe energy phenomena of the human organism, such terms as "warmth, pressure, tingling, vibration" etc. All

of these sensations refer to the sense of touch. One can first build the sensitivity of the sense of touch and then use the skills learned to feel energy.

Many bodywork therapies have exercises to build sensitivity of the hands. Consider taking seminars in massage or other bodywork techniques to build this sensitivity as well. An exercise that can be done with oneself or with a partner involves learning to discriminate layers of body tissue on the forearm and hand. First, gently attend to your breathing and make it diaphragmatic to center yourself a bit. Then use the fingertips or palm of the hand to feel the skin layer of your own or your partner's forearm. Try to move the skin a little bit, but move it so that only the skin moves and not the tissue layers under the skin. If you have trouble doing this at first, try the technique on the back of the hand where the skin is less firmly attached to the tissue layers under it.

After you are comfortable that you are moving only skin, then try to also move the layer between the skin and the more firm muscle that can be felt deep in the forearm. Try to become familiar with at least three distinct transitions in tissue layers from skin, subcutaneous layer (under skin, but not muscle), and muscle. Once comfortable distinguishing these layers, you might also want to feel for the bones of the forearm and see if you can follow the course of these bones throughout the length of the forearm.

There are also class offerings that teach energy perception. Health professionals can find therapeutic touch classes in many nursing schools. There may also be schools of therapeutic massage which offer courses in craniosacral therapy, shiatsu, reiki, and other treatment methods involving energy.

2. One can also practice feeling energy on oneself or on a partner. Most people find it initially easier to practice feeling energy on others before feeling their own energy centers. Sometimes people try to feel energy inside the body. One can frustrate oneself for a long time trying to feel energy centers somewhere in the spine, for example. Please keep in mind that energy centers have not only a center, but also radiance that can be felt a long way from the center. The origination point of a cakra, the bindu, is a null or void capable of being perceived and penetrated only after suṣumnā awareness has been established. When first trying to learn energy perception, it is usually easiest to feel the energetic radiance of a cakra with the hands away from the body rather than while touching the body.

Have your partner stand up and then position yourself to one side of them. Center yourself with the breath and, if needed, rub the fingertips of one hand back and forth over the palm and fingers of the opposite hand to get the mind to attend to your sense of touch.

One of the easiest energy centers to feel is located at the level of the navel. Establish diaphragmatic breathing as previously taught and place one hand somewhere between four and eighteen inches from your partner's navel. Similarly, place your other hand four to eighteen inches behind your partners back at the level of the navel. Adjust the distance between the two hands until you feel a pressure sensation, a resonance between the two hands. This will be your partner's energy center as perceived by your mind through your sense of touch. It is the interface of the energy field of your palms with your partner's navel center (maṇipūra cakra). The distance of the hand from the back does not necessarily have to be equal to the distance of the hand from the navel. Energy centers (cakras) can be felt at any distance depending on the radiance of the cakra and the focus of the observer.

Be respectful when working with energy awareness to prevent harm to oneself or others. Please do not attempt to push, pull or do things to someone's energy center until trained in one or more therapeutic methods involving energy work. Once there is confidence in the ability to feel something at the level of the navel, bring the hands up to the level of the heart center (anāhata cakra) at the midline of the chest where the lower ribs join the sternum (breastbone). Again position the hands four to eighteen inches from the front and back at this level until a resonance of pressure can be felt between the hands.

When confidence is gained at this level, move the hands upward to the level of the throat and feel the throat cakra (viśuddha cakra) in a similar manner. Learn to distinguish at least these three cakras with confidence. The shapes of cakras in the skull area are quite different than the lower cakras and awareness of them is best taught in person.

Something to consider:

Students sometimes wonder how yoga masters keep track of their students and their students' practice from a distance. Part of the answer to this question showed itself one day in a very personal way. My father was very scientifically minded and was always looking at physics and chemistry and physiological explanations for things. He had been born in 1897 and had seen the first automobile, the first airplane, the first motorcycle, etc. I remember saying a prayer for him every night for about three years. I said "I want him to have a glimpse of something beyond the scientific model, beyond the physiological model. Before he dies, I want him to experience something of consciousness not explained by the scientific."

One day I was attending a lecture in Honesdale, Pennsylvania given by my father's spiritual master, Swami Rama. Swamiji broke off his lecture, came over and stood beside me, and proceeded to tell the audience a story about my father. He spoke of a scientifically unexplainable glimpse of something my father had witnessed. My mother later verified the story, but she also added the more amazing details of material translocation left out of the public lecture. At the time Swamiji told us the story that day, I knew my father had had his glimpse beyond science. I also knew that my father was dying when that story was told. Twenty minutes later the message came that my father had collapsed from a cerebral hemorrhage at a place of business in Minneapolis. He had then been taken to an emergency room, with subsequent calls to my mother and then to Pennsylvania. It was clear that there is a level of contact possible between human beings that does not depend on current scientific knowledge or mechanical methods of communication. It was also clear that Swami Rama knew my prayer for my father and blessed me by demonstrating the answer to that prayer for my own knowledge as well as having graced my father with a glimpse beyond science during his lifetime.

As Yogi Achala, another student of Swami Rama, said at a conference in Minneapolis many years ago, "This tradition teaches in silence." Swami Rama didn't say to me, "Because of XYZ your prayers have been answered." The beautiful silence of personal experience began to teach me the sacred link that we all share. Our awareness can be individualized and personal, but our awareness can also be expanded and connected with all that is related to us.

XXVII. By performing saṃyama on the sun - knowledge of the solar system.

There is much archaeological evidence in the world that ancient cultures had significant knowledge of astronomy without the refined scientific instruments available today.

In this and the following sūtra it is uncertain whether the sūtras refer to the physical sun and moon or to the solar and lunar energy channels of piṅgalā and iḍā.

Something to consider:

If performing saṃyama on the sun yields knowledge of the solar system, then does performing saṃyama on sun or solar energy within us lead to knowledge of sūrya vidyā, the solar science?

XXVIII. By performing saṃyama on the moon - knowledge concerning the arrangement of stars.

Something to consider:

If performing saṃyama on the moon yields knowledge regarding arrangement of the stars, does performing saṃyama on the lunar energy within us lead to knowledge of the system of energy points and the connection of those points within?

XXIX. By performing saṃyama on the polestar - knowledge of the movement of the stars.

A broader interpretation of this sūtra is that by performing saṃyama on any fixed point, one can understand movement relative to that point. A broader understanding of laws of physics without dependence on scientific instrumentation can be possible.

XXX. By performing saṃyama on the navel plexus - knowledge of the body.

Not only is the knowledge of internal anatomy possible, but also the knowledge of its physiological makeup and the ability to put oneself back in balance.

XXXI. By performing saṃyama on the throat well (pit of the throat) - cessation of hunger and thirst.

There are reports of yogis who have not had anything to eat or drink for years. Keep in mind there may be other benefits and abilities related to focusing on the cakras than those few described in the Yoga Sūtras.

XXXII. By performing saṃyama on kūrma nādī - steadiness, motionlessness or immovability.

Kūrma nādī is described as a tortoise-shaped energetic tube below the throat cakra. When beginning one's meditation, it can be helpful after one has a balanced the left and right energies to spend a little time focusing on this energetic tube in order to stabilize one's posture. Remember that the quality (texture) of the element of space or ether associated with viśuddha cakra is absolute stillness.

Practice:

To gain experience in locating kūrma nādī, one can do the following practice. Once one has found the energy orb in the indentation above the upper lip (the practice presented in Sādhanā Pāda, XLIX) look for a tunnel of energy leading downward. While waiting for awareness of the tunnel, my teacher advised becoming aware of the mantra "soham" to be timed with the breath. "So" is the mental focus on the inhale and "ham" on the exhale. Put the vibration of the mantra at the indentation above the upper lip and see where that vibration wishes to flow in time with the breath. Let the tunnel lead you to that area behind the sternum just below the pit of the throat.

Something to consider:

Even without the performance of saṃyama, the steadiness of any pose in yoga can be improved by attending to the prāṇas while performing the pose. Bringing one's perception to the level of the prāṇas in āsana practice will provide a new dimension of experience for the practitioner.

XXXIII. By performing saṃyama on the light under the crown of the head - vision of perfected beings, adepts.

The artistic representations of sahasrāra cakra are as varied in number as the number of artists portraying this cakra. Artistic representations with the viewpoint outside of the skull often attempt to portray the description of a thousand-petaled lotus.

One summer in the early 1990s, my teacher had just finished lecturing at a conference in Chicago. I happened to be reading a book on a sofa by the back door of the hotel after the conclusion of the conference. I saw my teacher coming through that area of the hotel to depart. When I stood up, he came over to me and asked when I would be coming to Honesdale (national headquarters of the Himalayan Institute). There was a weeklong seminar to be given there that summer. I said I was coming to "Saundaryalahari", the title of the seminar. My teacher laughed as he put his hand on my shoulder before leaving for the airport.

At the seminar the meaning of his laughter became clear. Following a lecture given by my teacher, I went up to my room to do my customary śavāsana prior to lunch. My senses withdrew as the world tuned out, a familiar feeling to me indicating that a state of samādhi was coming. As suṣumnā awareness was established, a veil of color became visible with the tactile sensation of an energetic gateway on the forehead. Maintaining suṣumnā awareness, the veil of light appeared to come closer, making clear the pattern of light from which the veil was formed. A number of mantras that I had been practicing came into awareness almost simultaneously as my consciousness passed through one of the dark areas in the veil of color. It was as if consciousness was passing through a hole in the screen door, the wires of the screen being made up of a pattern of light. Beyond the veil was a nādī, dark in the interior and bordered by a pattern of light. This nādī led to some choices, the continuation of the nādī and some doorways. One of the choices led to a view of sahasrāra cakra from below. The initial presentation resembled the sun rising over the waves of an ocean. As suṣumnā awareness was maintained, the true nature of that ocean and its waves became clear. Saundarya-lahari is a place where one can witness the union of a single aspect of divine potential above with the force of creation from the abode of Śakti below. That union resembles lightning in that it results in a profound silence. Following the absolute silence, there is a rush to fill that silence much like the air that rushes in to fill the vacuum created by lightning. The rush to fill the silence of the void sets up a vibration that becomes something revealed.

XXXIV. Everything from intuition.

Merging one's awareness to become one with that which one is trying to understand results in complete, intuitive knowledge of that which one is trying to understand. In his commentary on the Yoga Sūtras, Swami Satchidananda states that all the siddhis come by themselves. One does not need to chase after them. As one practices and becomes more familiar with the three components of saṃyama (dhāraṇā, dhyāna, and samādhi), the meanings of the sutras in Vibhūti Pada become clearer.

XXXV. Saṃyama on the heart (cakra) - awareness of the mind.

One obtains knowledge of citta, all the impressions in the mind. Remember that everything in the universe is stored as an impression in the mind. All the impressions in the mind with their associated feelings and prāṇas that continue to create waves in the mind can be clearly perceived.

XXXVI. Intuition results from removing the distinction between the observer and the observed.

While performing saṃyama on a content of the mind being studied, one can surrender one's sense of I-am-ness and merge awareness with that which is being studied, experiencing the object of study as it experiences itself. As with many of the sutras, scholars will vary on their translation and interpretation. To truly understand this sutra, one must experience the process described in this sūtra. One must have the courage and steadiness to temporarily surrender one's personal sense of identity and assume the identity of the object of study.

XXXVII. From the knowledge of sutra thirty-six are produced intuitional hearing, touch, sight, taste and smell.

The gross sense organs are not actually needed for intuitive knowledge. The practitioner has superphysical senses in that knowledge of the object of study is obtained by directly experiencing, merging one's consciousness with the object of study. The practitioner is not required to analyze sensory data provided by sense organs in order to have such knowledge.

XXXVIII. In samādhi, siddhis are obstacles.

While the siddhis may assist in the performance of one's duties in the world, attachment to those same siddhis are considered obstacles in the practitioner's progress toward seedless samādhi.

XXXIX. The mind can enter another's body on relaxation of the cause of bondage of mind to body and by knowledge of the passages.

Commentators sometimes referred to citta-vāhā-nādī as the passage by which the mind can enter and leave the body. This sūtra presumes the practitioner already has knowledge of that which connects mind and body. It is assumed the practitioner is able to focus directly on the prāṇas and understands the vehicle of conveyance of impressions of the mind as well as the channels through which they might travel. The ability described in this sūtra is of particular value in the tradition of teaching or learning in silence. In such a relationship with a teacher, consciousness is shared at times.

XL. Mastery over udāna - levitation.

Besides the ability to levitate, some commentators state that mastery over this upward flowing prāṇa can result in one's ability to leave the body at will.

XLI. Mastery over samāna - blazing of gastric fire or radiance.

Samāna prāṇa is that energy gathered at maṇipūra cakra through various practices including āsana, prāṇayāma, and focusing of consciousness. There is a quality of radiance surrounding the yogi who has mastered samāna prāṇa. This radiance may be tactile or visual. There are yogis who can demonstrate a photographically verifiable radiance of light when focusing upon particular prāṇas and cakras.

XLII. Saṃyama on the relation of ākāśa (space or ether) and the ear results in superphysical hearing.

Remember that ākāśa, the element ether, is that which is capable of accepting a vibration in order to manifest as something perceivable by the senses.

XLIII. Saṃyama on the relation between body and ākāśa while bringing about coalescence of body with lightness gives the power of passage through space.

The body is formed as a combination of textures of the elements of earth, water, fire, and air within a particular space. Intuitive understanding of the relationship of the body and ākāśa allows the practitioner to add the texture of lightness within that space occupied by the body. One is specifically combining and merging the principle or quality of lightness (such as the lightness of the cotton fiber floating in the air) as an additional texture to be added to that space (ākāśa) occupied by the body.

XLIV. By saṃyama on the state of consciousness outside the intellect, sometimes referred to as mahā-videhā (the power of getting outside of one's own intellect), is destroyed the covering of light.

The practitioner transcends the individual mind and sense organs in perception of that which the practitioner is trying to understand. This is part of the process of intuitive knowledge, particularly when it involves merging awareness with the Divine.

XLV. One obtains mastery over the bhūtas (five elements) by performing saṃyama on their gross (the manifest form perceivable by the senses), subtle (vibratory characteristics or textures), all-pervading (constant or potential) and functional (interactional with each other according to natural laws) states.

This sūtra indicates the ability of the practitioner to be able to transmute or transform admixtures of the elements, an ability that is part of many of the practices in the tantric traditions. A particular space has the element of ether, an element with the quality of stillness capable of accepting vibration to assume a particular texture and gross form perceivable by the senses. Just as energy can organize to form particles of atoms (or form atoms, molecules, solids, liquids, gases, etc.) vibrations of energy organize to form textures of the elements. Understanding the subtle energies and vibrations that contribute to the textures of earth, water, fire, and air and understanding how to combine those textures allows one to fill a particular space with that interaction of textures. That space then becomes manifest with that particular combination of textures. Performing saṃyama helps to bring this about as it allows the practitioner to hold the combination of textures in that space through the breaks that naturally occur many times per second as the universe reabsorbs and remanifests itself. The manifest universe, after all, is the blending of textures of the elements within a particular space that just happens to be infinite. The universe has a vibratory nature just as do the elements of earth, water, fire, and air.

XLVI. The ability presented in sūtra XLV leads to the eight siddhis.

The eight siddhis are: 1) Aṅiman, becoming very small; 2) Mahiman, becoming very large; 3)Laghiman, becoming very light; 4) Gariman, becoming very heavy; 5)Prāpti, to be able to reach everywhere; 6) Prākāmya, to achieve all of one's desires; 7)Īśatva, to create anything; 8) Vaśitva, to be able to command and control everything.

XLVII. Beauty, fine complexion, gracefulness, strength and adamantine hardness constitute perfections of the body.

Mastery of the elements leads to the outward reflection of perfection of the body in its manifest form. This would include perfect health as internal organization or cohesion of the elements in accordance with natural law allows the perfection of constitutional strength. Constitution is that aspect of the human organism that allows oneself to remain in balance despite stressors that would otherwise put one out of balance.

XLVIII. By performing saṃyama over the senses, their real nature, their power of cognition or sensing, their all-pervasiveness, their seeming personal nature (egoism or sense of I-am-ness), and their functions, one obtains mastery over the sense organs.

Mastering the senses is important to balance one's responses to that which appears in one's meditation practice. When the guides appear in one's meditation, maintaining physiological, mental, and emotional balance enables steadiness in the presence of their appearance and is helpful should one decide to merge with their consciousness.

This same steadiness also allows balance to be maintained when receiving sensory input during everyday life. Without such balance, it is difficult to achieve the ideals outlined by the yamas and the niyamas.

XLIX. Through the mastery indicated by sūtra forty-three comes the instantaneous cognition without the vehicle of

the senses and complete mastery of pradhāna (the creative energy of the Puruṣa).

The phrase vikarana-bhāva in this sūtra means not only does the practitioner have the ability to know something without using the senses, but also has the ability to act without using any instrument such as the active senses (speaking, grasping, moving, reproducing, and elimination). The accomplished yogi can perceive anything anywhere in the manifest universe without the aid of the senses and fully understand it instantly. To create change in the manifest universe without action of any kind also becomes possible.

L. From the awareness of the distinction between sattva (the pure reflective nature) and Puruṣa (the true Self) arises supremacy over all states and forms of existence - omnipotence and omniscience.

Omniscience and omnipotence by their very nature are unlimited and cannot function through a vehicle which is limited. One must recognize oneself as different from the power or vehicle of perception.

LI. By nonattachment to that (referred to in sūtra fifty), the very seed of bondage is destroyed resulting in kaivalya (liberation).

Just as using possessions in the service of others, the siddhis are used in the service of others to free one from the bondage of karma and attachment to the manifest universe.

Something to consider:

When you obtain the siddhis, how will you choose to relate to them?

LII. There should be avoidance of pleasure or pride and being invited by super physical entities in charge of various planes as the possibility of revival of evil can result.

There is a reason the concept of fallen ones exists in various cultures. Just as sensory pleasures of the world can entice the senses, the power of the siddhis can entice the ego. There is a reason human beings are trapped in the cycle of birth and death. It is perhaps a similar reason that the world currently appears trapped in the cycle of yugas (repeating eons).

LIII. Performing saṃyama on the moment in its process of progression (time) leads to knowledge born of awareness of reality.

Moments that occur many times per second between the reabsorption and reappearance of the vibratory nature of the universe present opportunities for that universe to change course. It is within these moments one has the capacity to exert free will, to change the subsequent reappearance of the universe. Mastery of those clouded moments between reabsorption and reappearance leads to the knowledge of who one really is and the ability to exercise that free will. One is no longer bound by the destiny dictated in part by time.

LIV. From it (sūtra fifty-three) comes knowledge of the distinction between similars which cannot be distinguished by class, characteristic, or position.

There is an intersection of many directions and factors leading into and branching out from a moment in time. The yogi who has gained the capacity to distinguish what has been reabsorbed prior to a moment in time from that which appears subsequent to that moment of time gains mastery over that moment of time. Through that mastery a yogi then has the capacity to influence what otherwise might branch out from a moment in time. Such capacity to influence the future is an aspect of free will.

Something to consider:

Astrologers attempt to divine what tendencies and/or events are likely to occur at a future time. When the energies are shifted by such events as an experience of samādhi, an initiation by a master, or a revelation obtained unbound by the moments of time, then predestination no longer applies. Such events have the capacity to shift the vibratory reappearance of the universe.

LV. The highest knowledge, that which is beyond time, space, and causation, allows holding in awareness all objects simultaneously.

The barrier in the mind between that which is ordinarily conscious and that which is ordinarily unconscious is dissolved. Consciousness has access to everything without the limitations provided by the individual mind.

LVI. Kaivalya (liberation) is attained when there is equality of purity between Puruṣa and sattva. Sattva is then free from the illusion of identity.

The individual self no longer sees oneself as separate from the true Self.

Kaivalya Pāda

I. Siddhis are the result of birth, herbs, mantras, austerities, or samādhi.

As a result of experiences and practices prior to birth, one might receive a siddhi based on that prior experience. One might also receive access to a siddhi based on an experience with a drug or herb. Unfortunately in both of these circumstances, one is not necessarily prepared for the impact of that siddhi. This can lead to an imbalance in life and actually be an obstacle to the path of yoga.

Mantra japa might also lead to a result involving a siddhi. Mantras are sometimes given by a master to achieve a specific result. This is different from trying to practice the mantra after having read the mantra in a book somewhere. One must not underestimate the energetic shift that occurs when a practice is given with the accompanying grace of Śakti.

There is an ancient saying "When the student is ready, the teacher will come." This does not mean that one has to run around the world looking for a guru. When the student has undertaken the practices to prepare and is then ready, the masters who are manifest as well as unmanifest are drawn to the student to help provide that grace of Śakti.

"Austerities" in the context of this sūtra means gaining willpower over the mind and its tendencies. Both mantra japa and the austerities tend to mold the energy of the student and prepare that student for receiving that grace of energy called Śakti.

Samādhi is part of that practice previously defined as saṃyama from which many siddhis can result.

Something to consider:

Just as sūtra XLVI in Sādhanā Pada states that postures should be comfortable and steady, the idea of discipline in regard to austerities of practice needs to be understood. Discipline grooves the mind and body in doing the specific practices of yoga. Not attending to capacity can result in imbalance and injury.

An example regarding capacity would be length of practice of diaphragmatic breathing and mantra japa. My teacher would advise to sit every day for one's practice, but also advised that total concentration for three breaths was worth more than twenty minutes of the mind running elsewhere while doing breathing or mantra japa. I tell my students to practice each day but only for as long as the practice holds their interest. If a practice is not holding the interest of the student, or is not enjoyed, it may be beyond the student's capacity. A different practice may be more beneficial for them. Balancing determination, enjoyment, and capacity are keys to progress on the path of yoga.

Something to consider:

Does your practice feel balanced? Do you enjoy it? From time to time, examine your practice to see if it feels balanced.

II. Transformation of one species into another is by overflow or inflow of natural tendencies or potentialities.

Some will interpret this sūtra as Darwin's law of natural selection. Philosophers and religious scholars can argue about this. If this sūtra is taken in the context of the previous sūtra, transformation refers to the change occurring from birth to birth, not to Darwin's law of natural selection.

My teacher used to say that what separates human beings from animal species is the ability to reason. Karmas from time to time may determine that the student's best option for learning or changing habits might be to be born as a species without that ability to reason.

III. Incidental cause does not move or stir up natural tendencies, but merely removes the obstacles, like a farmer.

Removal of obstacles is part of the path of grace. The guiding light of this universe, or guru as it is sometimes termed, does not do the work of evolving consciousness for you. When you have prepared yourself with the preliminary practices, a gateway is simply opened by that guiding light called guru. The next step in your development on the path of yoga then comes into view. Like the farmer opening an irrigation sluice gate so that water might enter the field and nourish the plants, preparation allows for the removal of obstacles on the path of yoga.

You already have the potential or "natural tendency" to reach the goal of yoga. It is the removal of obstacles by preparation and by grace that allows growth toward that goal.

IV. Artificially created minds proceed from egoism alone.

The Divine Self is the potential for all possible individual minds before a spark of it is wrapped in layers and layers of ignorance to become a human soul. The principle of I-am-ness (ego) leads to the creation of individual minds.

V. The one mind is the director of the many artificial minds.

The Divine Self is the potential for all the individual minds, including the minds of all of one's births.

VI. Of these individual minds, the mind born of meditation is free of impressions.

If one has gained the ability to achieve that perfect one-pointed focus that is the goal of meditation, it is possible to be born free of the saṃskāras or impressions that would otherwise have been present because of past karmas. The seeds of these impressions no longer have the energy attached that would push them forward in the mind.

VII. Karma is not white or black for a yogi, but is threefold for others.

Actions of a yogi do not give rise to good or bad karma as they do not result in any karma. For one who has not yet achieved the goal of yoga, the results or fruits of one's actions may be good, bad, or mixed. Mixed, in this context, refers to actions that might be undertaken with good intent but somehow led to a harmful result. For example, choosing to vaccinate one's child in order to improve the child's health would be an action undertaken with good intent. If the child has a reaction to the vaccine requiring medical attention, the result of a well-intended action caused some harm.

VIII. Only tendencies are manifested for which conditions are favorable.

Vāsanās (subconscious impressions) lie dormant in the mind until conditions are favorable for one to work on the karmas. On a more surface level, unconscious impressions can push forward to influence our dreams, feelings, and thinking in this life. On a deeper level, the obstacles and opportunities that we might face in our birth circumstance are part of what is referred to in this sūtra.

IX. Memory and impressions are the same in form even though separated by class, locality, and time.

To understand this sūtra, it is assumed the student understands the concept of reincarnation. Vāsanās are of the same form on a subtle energetic level. They may be separated in terms of time of formation, where they were formed, and in which lifetime. They are part of oneself that is carried from lifetime to lifetime through the process of birth and death.

X. The process is eternal as there is no beginning to the desire to live.

The innate desire of human beings to answer the questions of who we are, from where have we come, to where are we going, that desire to become aware of who we truly are, is inborn and inescapable. Life is the arena in which one prepares to receive the answers to these questions.

XI. Vāsanās disappear only on disappearance of their cause.

The "cause" referred to in this sūtra is avidyā, or lack of knowledge. As described in the previous sutras, vāsanās serve to direct one's life toward attaining knowledge of the true Self.

XII. Past and future exist in real form because of the differences in dharmas (conditions or properties), the difference in paths.

The term "dharma" has many definitions. It can have as its meaning virtue or righteousness (as in a way of living or path of life), attribute, characteristic, quality, etc. Each individual has a particular set of vāsanās, karmas, and individual boundaries between that which is conscious and that which is unconscious in the mind. These conditions and properties influence the path that one's life takes through time.

In an expanded context, the collective needs of all humankind are the obstacles and opportunities needed to be faced to resolve the karmas and vāsanās of all. These determine the world's path through time. In the yogic view, the world is the collection of the obstacles and opportunities from which we need to learn, both individually and collectively. The world is nothing more than that. It is nothing less than that.

Something to consider:

What do you consider your path in the world to be? How will your path influence the path of the world through time?

XIII. The properties (dharma) manifest or unmanifest are the nature of guṇas (tendencies).

The guṇas are the tendencies or forces that determine the general trend of the reappearance of the universe for the next moment in time. The universe, with its vibratory nature of reabsorption and reappearance many times per second, has its reappearance determined by what humanity collectively needs to remove the layers of ignorance around the true Self.

XIV. The essence of an object consists in the uniqueness of transformation (of the guṇas).

Whether the object is small like a single orange or large like the world, the uniqueness of organization of the energies and vibrations are the essence of that object.

XV. Different minds (with different paths or dharmas) perceive the same object differently.

When coming to know an object like an orange, one person might be struck by the color and the texture of the rind around the orange. Another might immediately peel and bite into the orange and be struck by the sweetness of its taste. Someone in the same room might note the fragrance of the orange that has been peeled. Each individual mind has a unique experience of that orange.

Similarly the boundaries of awareness of each individual mind influence what aspects of the world are observed in any given moment. The world at that moment is the same, but the experience of the world as well as of the smaller objects of the world can differ for each individual mind.

XVI. An object of the world does not depend upon one mind for its existence. What would become of the object if it were not cognized by an individual mind?

Objects of the world are part of the collective mind, part of the world. They are not the product of any individual mind. The forest is still there even if one is not walking through the forest and appreciating it at any given moment. The islands of Hawaii are still present even for those who have never been there.

XVII. If an object "colors" the mind (leaves an impression in the mind) it is known, otherwise it is not known.

While everything in the universe has a vibratory quality and leaves an energetic imprint, those impressions can be left to be sensed and appreciated by the conscious mind, or can leave an impression in the unconscious mind. Everything in the universe leaves an impression of some kind. If it does not leave an impression in your conscious or unconscious mind, it does not exist.

Another aspect of this sūtra is that for an object to be appreciated and understood by the mind, that object must first leave an impression in the mind. The mind can then become aware of the object in order to study it.

XVIII. Modifications of the mind are always known by its Lord.

Even though the individual mind may not be aware consciously of an object of the world, the non-dynamic aspect of Self will be aware of that object. On some level, one is always conscious of everything, the non-dynamic aspect of Self is knowing fully what is both in the conscious as well as the unconscious parts of the mind.

XIX. Because it is perceptible, the mind is not self-luminous.

The mind is a reflection of the true Self. Just as the moon is seen in the sky because of being illuminated by the sun, the mind can only be understood fully by being illuminated by the consciousness of the true Self. If the mind tries to understand itself, it only follows its perceptions, thoughts, and feelings and cannot experience the entirety of itself.

XX. The mind can't be the perceiver and the perceived at the same time.

The mind cannot perceive itself while it still has the boundaries of the mind separating what is conscious from that which is unconscious. The mind cannot be fully conscious of itself because of its nature to have conscious and unconscious aspects.

XXI. If one tries to cognize the mind by another (mind), there will be cognition of cognitions and confusion of memories.

If one tries to know the limited mind with a limited mind, there will not be complete knowledge. An example of this principle would be trying to use an instrument such as a psychological test to fully understand the mind. Knowledge of the mind is incomplete as only clues for interpretation are obtained with such a limited instrument being used to study the mind. There may be some clues obtained about unconscious impressions, but the entirety of the mind, both conscious and unconscious, will not be known.

Another example would be if one were try to understand the taste of an orange while watching someone else eat the orange. One would have no direct experience with the taste of an orange and knowledge of the taste would be incomplete.

If one tries to understand the entirety of one's own mind with a mind that has limited knowledge of itself, understanding will not be complete.

XXII. The mind attains knowledge of its own nature through self-cognition when consciousness assumes that form in which it does not pass from place to place.

When the mind itself becomes non-dynamic through citta-vṛitti-nirodha, absence of fluctuations of the mind stuff, the mind then achieves a non-dynamic perspective. The mind becomes a reflection of the true Divine Self from which the soul becomes manifest. The mind takes a viewpoint without fluctuation to cognize that aspect of oneself that is without fluctuation. The practices of yoga are designed to lead consciousness to that non-dynamic perspective.

XXIII. The mind colored by the knower (Puruṣa) and the known is all-apprehending.

The boundaries of ignorance that separate the conscious from the unconscious mind are eliminated as the true Self is merged with the mind. One then has intuitive understanding of the true Self. In other words, consciousness is aware of the entirety of oneself, including that divine potential for all things as being part of oneself.

XXIV. Mind, though variegated and colored by innumerable vāsanās, the mind acts for another (Puruṣa), for it acts in association with Puruṣa.

The mind acts in service of the whole, not in service of the ego (I-am-ness).

XXV. One has the cessation of desire for dwelling in the consciousness of ātmā for one who has seen the distinction.

Thoughts of the mind desiring to be an individual self cease forever.

Something to consider:

When you achieve such a state, will you choose to be born? Why or why not?

XXVI. Then the mind is inclined toward discrimination and gravitating towards kaivalya.

The mind prefers to dwell in its own true nature, liberating the mind from its ignorance and the tendency to maintain that ignorance.

XXVII. In the intervals arise other pratyayas from the force of saṃskāras.

Pratyayas are ideas and experiences that present themselves to an aspect of mind so that cognition may occur. The universe still maintains its vibratory nature, reabsorbing and reappearing many times per second. Remember that the field of karma is not simply an individual concern, but a collective concern as well. As long as the world continues to be needed by humanity, saṃskāras of those still treading the path influence the path the world takes moment to moment through time. With sufficient force and magnitude, there is a chance of rebirth, life then being an interval from kaivalya.

XXVIII. Their removal (of the pratyayas), like that of kleśas, has been described.

The removal of kleśas was described in Samādhi Pada, sūtras I, II, X, XI, and XXVI. The obstacles become quiescent. The yogi may still choose to be born in further service of the whole, but is not attached to that choice to be born.

XXIX. For one who is able to maintain a constant state of vairāgya even towards the most exalted state of enlightenment and to exercise the highest kind of discrimination then follows Dharma-Megha-Samādhi.

Dharma-Megha-Samādhi refers to consciousness dwelling in that samādhi where all the beautiful or virtuous qualities of Dharma are in awareness as well as knowledge of the nature of all things.

XXX. Then follows freedom from kleśas and karmas.

All that affects the mind, trying to push it away from that awareness of the Divine, ceases.

XXXI. In consequence of the removal of all obscurations and impurities, that which can be known through the mind is but little in comparison with the infinity of knowledge.

XXXII. The three guṇas having fulfilled their objective, the process of change comes to an end.

Something to consider:

Is there some point and condition required where the world no longer needs to exist?

XXXIII. The process corresponding to moments (kṣaṇa) which become apprehensible at the end of transformation of the guṇas is kramaḥ.

XXXIV. Kaivalya is the state following re-mergence of the guṇas because of their becoming void of the object of the Puruṣa. In this state the Puruṣa is established in its Real or Divine nature which is pure consciousness (non-dynamic).

Something to consider:

If an aspect of self is still changing, namely those still treading the path toward the infinity of knowledge, can one still be unchanging except regarding one's potentials (non-dynamic aspect of Self)? If the universe is indeed infinite, is it not capable of infinite evolution? After a re-mergence of the guṇas, does the universe then have the choice to evolve into a form not yet known? Is there no longer a need for yugas? Are we here to participate in the process of evolution? Are we created to arrive at a final answer or goal in life?

Glossary

abhiniveśa	desire for life sustained by its own potency
abhyāsa	practice, as in sustained effort
ahaṃkāra	ego; sense of individual I-am-ness
ahiṃsā	non-harming; nonviolence
āliṅga	as yet without differentiation or characteristics
anāhata cakra	heart center
aparigraha	non-acquisitiveness
asaṃprajñāta	A state of total insight not requiring supportive factors such as an object of focus
āsanas	yoga poses
asmitā	Blending together of the power of pure consciousness with the power of cognition; the one who apprehends
asteya	non-stealing
ātman	divine spark that is part of the individual soul
avidyā	lack of knowledge
aviśeṣa	universal or non-specific
bhāvanā	dwelling upon in the mind, cultivating and absorbing a meaning
bhūtas	elements; earth, water, fire, air, ether or space

bīja	seed
brahmacarya	walking the path of Brahman
buddhi	discriminative faculty of the mind
citta-vṛitti	storehouse of impressions of the mind
citta-vṛitti-nirodha	silence of the waves of the mind
dhāranā	concentration
dharma	condition or property; attribute
dharmī	property holder, the nature or that which is the thing in past, present, and future forms
dhyāna	meditation
dveṣaḥ	repulsion that accompanies pain
ekāgratā	one-pointedness of mind
ekāgratā pariṅāma	one-pointedness on a temporary state of mind
guṇas	tendencies that are part of the process of manifestation
Haṃsa	That I am; swan as a symbol of the source of oneself
hatha	solar-lunar; right-left
iḍā	left or lunar energy channel
Iśvara	that divine consciousness untouched by the afflictions of life
Iśvara-praṇidhāna	Iśvara, the Divine; praṇidhāna, practicing in the presence of; surrendering to the presence of the Divine or self surrendering to Self

japa	systematic mental repetition of a mantra
kaivalya	self realization; liberated; isolation of the Self from all matter
karmas	actions (thought, words spoken, deeds) and their repercussions
kevala kumbhaka	suspension of the need to breath
kirtan	call and response devotional chanting intended to open the heart of participants to the Divine
kleśas	painful pollutants of the mind
kriya	preliminary or preparatory
kumbhaka	retention of breath
kuṇḍalinī	force of manifestation, feminine aspect of the Divine, first prāṇa
kūrma nādī	tortoise tube
liṅga – mātra	Identifier; such as fruit as an identifier for both an orange and an apple
maṇḍala	circle; art form for spiritual or ritual art
mantra	sound, series of sounds or phrases used in yoga practices
māyā	erroneous self- identification of being an individual
nādī	subtle energy channel or pathway
nādī ṣodhana	purification of the nervous system; alternate nostril breathing; purification of the nādīs

nidrā	sleep; of sleep
nirbīja	without seed
niyamas	observances; austerities for conducting life
pāda	foot, or footprint, one of four sections or parts
pariṅāma	temporary state of mind
piṅgalā	right or solar energy channel
Prakṛiti	universal nature, the manifest
prāṇa	subtle energy of any physical object or mental impression
prāṇāyāma	regulation of the subtle energies
pratyāhāra	withdrawal of the gross senses
pratyaya	seed or content of the mind at a given moment
Puruṣa	the potential for all, not yet manifest
rāgaḥ	attraction that accompanies pleasure
sabīja	with seed
sādhanā	a means of accomplishing something; discipline or practice
Śakti	force of manifestation; female aspect of the Divine
śaktipāta	an act of grace where the Divine energy serves to illuminate one in some way
samādhi	expanded state of consciousness

saṃprajñāta	total insight requiring supportive factors such as an object of focus
saṃskāra	impression in the mind
saṃtoṣa	contentment
saṃyama	simultaneous application of dhāranā, dhyāna, and samādhi
sānanda	sa, with or accompanied by, ānanda, rapture or bliss
sasmitā	sa, with or accompanied by, asmitā, I-am-ness
satya	truthfulness
śauca	purity
śavāsana	corpse pose
siddhis	attainments resulting from yoga practice
śīthalī karaṇa	progressively ascending breath
Śiva	divine potential; male aspect of the Divine
smṛti	mindfulness
soham	I am That; derivative of Haṃsa-mantra
sūrya vidyā	solar science
suṣumnā	central energy pathway
sūtra	thread; concise phrase or presentation
svādhyāya	self study leading to purification; study of one's own lesson
tapas	self-discipline; austerity
vairāgya	cessation of desires

vāsanā	subconscious impression
vibhūti	powerful expansions; sacred ash, results of preparation through yoga disciplines
vicāra	refined or subtle thought
vipāka	fruits of one's actions
viśeṣa	particular or specific
vitarka	thought accompanied by names of particular objects of focus; gross thought
vivek - khyātiḥ	knowledge of discrimination of the real from the unreal
vṛitti	modification of the mind; impression in the mind; wave of the mind; operation of the mind
yamas	attitudes with which to conduct one's life
yantra	three dimensional form of maṇḍala; an admixture of vibration or vibrations that assumes a three dimensional form
yoga	union; bind together or yoke
yuga	age or eon